# MAINE'S APPALACHIAN TRAIL

How Seniors Made Section Hiking Easier

by

Harvey A. Dennenberg a.k.a. GrandPa Walking

The contents of this work, including, but not limited to, the accuracy of events, people, and places depicted; opinions expressed; permission to use previously published materials included; and any advice given or actions advocated are solely the responsibility of the author, who assumes all liability for said work and indemnifies the publisher against any claims stemming from publication of the work.

All Rights Reserved
Copyright © 2022 by Harvey A Dennenberg a.k.a. GrandPa Walking

No part of this book may be reproduced or transmitted, downloaded, distributed, reverse engineered, or stored in or introduced into any information storage and retrieval system, in any form or by any means, including photocopying and recording, whether electronic or mechanical, now known or hereinafter invented without permission in writing from the publisher.

Dorrance Publishing Co
585 Alpha Drive
Suite 103
Pittsburgh, PA 15238
Visit our website at *www.dorrancebookstore.com*

ISBN: 978-1-6853-7000-8
eISBN: 978-1-6853-7857-8

# DEDICATION

I've been asked several times over the past few months about who I would dedicate my Maine Appalachian Trail (AT) story to and each time I've not been able to answer the question. Although I've hiked with thirty-two other hikers, mostly seniors and mostly men, I've actually only hiked the Appalachian Trail in Maine with eight other seniors. Pokey was the only lady.

Ron Filbert who helped me to complete my journey to Baxter Peak on Katahdin in 2011 was not only my first hiking partner but he was also the first hiker to respond to my first posting to hike the AT. He died from complications of skin cancer in June 2013. He was the first person to inspire me continue to hike the AT. Lee Holoman from Tennessee was also a great influence as he was the first to teach me how to plan a hike. He and Greg Peters of Florida were great influences in teaching me how to plan hikes over multiple days. This was critical in my planning my Maine Appalachian Trail hikes. Fred Firman of Pennsylvania advice on how to use terrain to decide a hiking direction was also critical influence for Maine. Fred's hiking notes and those of Ed Bocklage, also of Pennsylvania were influential in planning the direction, northbound or southbound, of a number of our hikes.

Ed Vrba, a.k.a. Joker whom I hiked Maine with since 2016 and Jim Lang, a.k.a. Chill whom I hiked Maine since 2017 were my constant companions for much of Maine's AT. Joker always led so he became the web breaker and Chill was always the Caboose to make sure I was OK. Chill helped locate some of the lesser-known access points to the Appalachian Trail and helped me to test drive a number of these access points in either my Subaru or one of his rental cars.

I also have to dedicate this book to Rattle River Lodging and Hostel in Shelburne New Hampshire. Marnie was the previous owner before she sold the Hostel to Erik Barstow. They both provide a lot of advice and suggestions on access roads to the AT and shuttles. Shaw's in Monson has supported me since I first stayed there in 2011 and its current owners, Poet and Hippy Chick provided advice to help me break up some of the more difficult sections in the Hundred Mile Wilderness along with their outstanding shuttle services. Old Man, owner of the AT Lodge in Millinocket and Hippy Chick's father provided outstanding shuttles to several places in the Hundred Mile Wilderness and his 6 A.M. morning shuttle to Baxter State Park helped us to complete the section out of Baxter State Park to the Golden Road. My appreciation and thanks go out to Honey at the Cabin in Andover who kept dinner ready for us even after we missed arriving at the time we were supposed to. The Caratunk House also provided great service and outstanding shuttles.

I also have to thank the Doctors and Physician Assistants (PA) who have helped me to get back into shape and stay in shape. Specifically, Doctor Angela Calle, Garrett Lee, PA-C, Michelle Pipta, PA-C, Meghan Bartlinski, DPT, CMTPT, Lauren Seidenstricker, PTA, and my Podiatrist Doctor Gene Mirkin. I also have to thank my Service Writer, Miguel Gochez and my Subaru mechanic, Frank Lamke at Wilkins Subaru for keeping my 2007 and then my 2010 Subaru Forester's in ship- shape condition. A special thanks to Tricia Spriggs my message therapist for the past ten years whose skill and advice helped me to stay in shape and avoid additional injuries. My five grandchildren were also a great influence and I always carrier their photo's with me when I section hiked.

My final dedication is to my wife and life partner, Madeleine, who is not an Appalachian Trail hiker, but supported me in spite of the cuts and bruises I brought back from a number of my Maine hikes. I could not have completed my hikes without her support. There are others who have helped but I never recorded their names in my notebooks.

# "NOTHING IS EASY ON MAINE'S APPALACHIAN TRAIL"
## – Author Unknown

Maine Painted Rock – Road to Baxter State Park

## TABLE OF CONTENTS

Chapter One: . . . . . . . . . . . . . . . . . . . . . . . . . . . . . . . . . . .1
    Background and History

Chapter Two: . . . . . . . . . . . . . . . . . . . . . . . . . . . . . . . . . .11
    Preparation and Training

Chapter Three: . . . . . . . . . . . . . . . . . . . . . . . . . . . . . . . .19
    Hiking Philosophy and Safety

Chapter Four: . . . . . . . . . . . . . . . . . . . . . . . . . . . . . . . . .23
    New Hampshire US Highway Two to Grafton Notch Maine Highway Twenty-Six

Chapter Five: . . . . . . . . . . . . . . . . . . . . . . . . . . . . . . . . .41
    Grafton Notch Maine Highway Twenty-Six to East Flagstaff Road

Chapter Six: . . . . . . . . . . . . . . . . . . . . . . . . . . . . . . . . . .67
    East Flagstaff Road to Monson Maine Highway Fifteen

Chapter Seven: . . . . . . . . . . . . . . . . . . . . . . . . . . . . . . . .81
    Hundred Mile Wilderness - Monson to Baxter State Park

Chapter Eight: . . . . . . . . . . . . . . . . . . . . . . . . . . . . . . . .113
    Conclusion and Statistics

# Chapter One
## Background and History
## Failures and Lessons for Success

On Friday, September 4th, 2009, I made a failed attempt to climb the Hunt Trail on the Appalachian Trail. It would have been a forty-two-hundred-foot (4200) climb over five-point-two (5.2) miles to Baxter Peak on Katahdin in Baxter State Park, near Millinocket, Maine. Before I discuss what went wrong and why, I believe it's important to explain what the Appalachian Trail is, but I will not discuss how it began as there are many great resources available today.

The Appalachian Trail, known as the AT, is twenty-one-hundred-ninety-three-point-one (2193.1) miles (according to AWOL Miller's *2021 Appalachian Trail Guide*). The Appalachian Trail runs through fourteen states, and the southern part of the Appalachian Trail begins at Springer Mountain near Suches and Dahlonega in Georgia. The northern point is on Baxter Peak on Katahdin in Baxter State Park near Millinocket, Maine.

Every year thousands of hikers attempt to hike the entire AT as a Thru Hike over a five- or six-month period, and less than twenty-five percent (25%) actually succeed. Originally a Thru Hike would be hiking the entire length of the AT either northbound from Springer Mountain Georgia or NoBo, or southbound from Baxter

Peak on Katahdin or SoBo in the same calendar year. Currently a Thru Hiker must complete the AT within a twelve-month period.

For those who cannot devote five or six months to hiking, hikers can choose to hike the AT in sections. My definition of a "section" might be part of a state or an entire state. It might be hiking a specific number of miles, or even hiking a specific number of consecutive days. For me a "section" can be a road to road day hike, or a two-day backpack and staying in a Shelter or tenting at a campsite.

The AT has Shelters, called Lean-to's in Maine, about every eight to ten miles. A shelter or Lean-to is a three-sided structure made of wood and sometimes stone with a slanted roof and open on one side. Most are one floor, but some have a second floor. Shelters or Lean-to's can accommodate anywhere from six to fourteen hikers. Most have access to a water source nearby and many but not all have a privy nearby. A privy or outhouse comes in many forms.

Now back to my story. On Thursday, September 3rd, 2009 I was in my sixty-eighth turn around the sun. I had just driven from Milwaukee, Wisconsin where I had celebrated my Fiftieth High School Reunion, via Toronto and Quebec in Canada, crossing into Maine and ending up in Millinocket, Maine. I had previously made reservations for three-nights at Katahdin Stream Campground in Baxter State Park as I felt I would need an extra day to hike the area before my climb up Katahdin and a day to recover after my climb.

I knew the Hunt Trail was five-point-two (5.2) miles and I'd be climbing forty-two hundred (4200) feet to Baxter Peak on Katahdin. At the time, I didn't have the *Appalachian Trail Data Book* nor AWOL Miller's *Appalachian Trail Guide*, and I didn't even have the terrain map for Baxter State Park and the Hunt Trail. I did have a compass.

Upon my arrival in Baxter State Park, I had just set up my old Coleman tent outside the Lean-to I had reserved when a young lady Ranger

Rachel came by and said I'd either have to sleep in the Lean-to or put my tent inside the Lean-to. She helped me do the latter. I spent the rest of that day walking on the trails around Katahdin Stream Campground, and I'm sure I hiked the AT south across some narrow wood bridges but not out of Baxter State Park.

On Friday, September 4th, around 6:55 A.M., I signed the log book at the beginning of the Hunt Trail on the AT and started my hike. The first mile to the bridge over Katahdin Stream Falls was very easy and fairly flat. A young Thru Hiker, Charlie, from Florida passed me just after I crossed the bridge over Katahdin Stream. By 11:30 A.M. I had hiked about three-point-two (3.2) miles and climbed thirty-four-hundred-fifty (3450) feet and somehow gotten up and over a huge boulder with the iron rebar embedded in the rock. Just beyond, I saw a white painted arrow and "2M" in white on a large rock.

**2009 Friday, September 4th, 11:30 A.M. Hunt Trail Baxter State Park**

**2009 Friday, September 4th, 11:30 A.M.
Hunt Trail Baxter State Park, Maine**

I could see ahead to the horizon and all I could see was a large open area filled with rock shale. Considering what I just had climbed and not knowing what lay ahead beyond the rock shale, I took stock that I was low on water and had less than one-half of my twenty-ounce Gatorade left. It had taken me four-point-five (4.5) hours to hike three-point-two (3.2) miles and didn't want to risk more climbs like I had just done and run out of water. Without a guide book or terrain map, I had no idea of what lay ahead.

What I didn't know at that time and this would be a "teaching moment". I only had six-hundred-thirty (630) feet of elevation to climb over the next two (2) miles and all the big, steep and tough climbs were behind me. I also feared that if I continued onto Baxter Peak I would have to climb back down in the dark. I took these photos, turned around and headed back down. On my way down, which took a lot more time, I realized how tired I was and I stopped many times to just sit and rest. Charlie, the young Thru Hiker who had passed me on the way up, stopped and asked if I was leaving Baxter today. I replied "Yes" and I told him where my Lean-to was. I said I'd give him a ride into Millinocket and treat him to dinner.

It was after 3 P.M. by the time I had crossed back over the wood bridge at Katahdin Stream Falls and I was totally out of water and Gatorade. The next mile was mostly flat and easy but it took me nearly an hour as I was exhausted and thirsty. It was just one step at a time for that last mile. When I got to the Lean-to, Charlie was there. I grabbed a gallon water jug and probably drank about half of it. Charlie helped me break down my tent and other gear and store it in my 2007 Subaru Forester.

We didn't talk as much during the drive into Millinocket. I was still very tired, probably exhausted too. Charlie wanted pizza and we shared a large shrimp pizza for dinner. I had two slices, he ate six. I felt much better after eating and drinking a Coke. I can count the number of soft drinks I drink in a year on one hand. Charlie said he needed to get to Bangor, Maine so he could fly home to Florida. I suggested there were probably better connections out of Portland, Maine. As we drove down Interstate Ninety-five (I-95) towards Portland it began to get dark. As the light of the day faded, I realized how exhausted I was and I said to Charlie that I needed to stop for the night. I spotted a Marriott sign and told Charlie I'd pay for his room. At the time I was a Marriott Gold card holder and I got us each a room at a good rate. Charlie went to his room and I used the computer in the lobby to verify that he could connect to Florida through Atlanta and the better flights were from Portland, Maine. The next morning I hardly recognized him as he had shaved his red beard. I only recognized him by his wild red hair. He lost his cell phone on the AT and he asked me for mine so he could speak with his mom. She agreed that the better connections to Florida were out of Portland.

Charlie doesn't like to fly and we ended up stopping at a couple of liquor stores where he bought several tiny bottles of liquor. As we pulled up to the Portland airport I slipped him twenty-dollars and said he should use the money to get something to eat in Atlanta as he had a long layover. We've remained email friends ever since. Charlie hiked the Pacific Crest Trail a couple of years later and I sent him a package along with money for beer. I asked him to buy Canadian beer when he finished in Canada. I got a photo from him later that year of him and the empty Canadian beer cans.

Between 2009 and through 2011 and beyond, I learned a number of valuable lessons. They all came from other more experienced hikers. Lee from Tennessee and Greg from Connecticut, now in Florida taught me how to plan a multi-day hike. Randy from Virginia and Lee from Tennessee taught me the two-car road to road hiking system. Fred F from Pennsylvania, Thru Hiked the AT in his fifties and then he hiked the AT again as a Section Hiker in his sixties. He also Section Hiked about seventy-percent (70%) of the AT for the third time in his seventies. He taught me about the ATC's terrain maps. Greg, taught me the importance of Garmin's GPS devices. Lee from Tennessee and Jim from New Jersey taught me how to find roads to access the Appalachian Trail that were not in AWOL's *AT Guide*. Ed B and Fred F, both from Pennsylvania taught me how to split up a group into fast and slower hikers, hiking in the opposite directions. I've also hiked with several women, Irene from Georgia and Jean from New Hampshire, Joan from Virginia, Pokey from Maine, and learned about their need for privacy. There were many positive lessons, and I choose to not dwell on the negative lessons learned except to say that I never made that particular mistake again. At least that's what I recall years later.

I've always preferred to hike with others and tried to find other seniors who would prefer to hike road to road or would prefer to limit the number of backpacking nights on the AT.

This is probably a good time to talk about backpacking. When you backpack, whether it be for one or two days or a week or more, you've got to carry everything you need for that period of time. The size of the backpack will determine how much you can or should carry and this is a very personal and a subjective choice. The essentials for backpacking are the pack, a sleeping bag and pad, a tent or hammock, water containers (plastic bottle(s), Platypus), water filtration or purification system, cooking stove, fuel for your stove, pot to cook in, spork to eat with, toilet paper, hand sanitizer, matches and/or lighter, small pocket knife, clothing, rain gear, breakfast-lunch-dinner-snacks for the number of hiking days. Boots or trail shoes, hiking poles, terrain maps, AT guide book, and compass. Last but not least is some form of communication device or Emergency beacon in case you have an emergency. Cell service can be non-existent in many places on the AT especially in parts of Maine and New Hampshire as well as in parts of other AT states. Far-Out, formerly Guthook, is a cell phone app that contains the entire AT. Jim, a.k.a. Chill introduced me to this app during our Maine and New Hampshire hikes. Equipment is very personal and I'll talk about how my choices changed over the years I've section hiked. Day hiking, or slacking, or slackpacking is a day pack and whatever food, water, and clothing you would need for a day hike.

In the late fall of 2009 I did my first Senior Hiker posting in the *Appalachian Trail Conservancy Magazine*. Since then I've hiked with thirty-two others, mostly seniors. Some once, some a few times and several for five or six years. Most of the time it's been with one or two others, mostly seniors. Once I organized a hike with six others. Yes, I never did that again. For each hike I plan, I created a day-by-day plan using an Excel Spreadsheet. In the past couple of years I also created a Word Doc with the same details, except for the GPS coordinates for each day we planned to hike. These documents allow my hiking partners to review the plan and to make sure I haven't made any mistakes or forgotten anything. Yes, I've made tons of mistakes and thankfully my partners caught them. We've also changed hiking directions a number of times after the initial plan, or the day of the actual hike.

Almost all AT Thru Hikers have "trail names". These are either given to them by other hikers or they choose their own name. Fred F, one of my best sources of information, is "Greybeard". Randy R is "Shady". Greg P is "Painted Turtle". I've even had the privilege of naming two young hikers from Germany a number of years ago that I met in Pennsylvania. I was originally "Caboose" as I was always the last in our hiking group, but "GrandPa Walking" is the real me.

2009 Friday, September 4th AT Hunt Trail climbed 2300 feet

# Chapter Two
## Preparation and Training

A critical factor for any senior who plans to hike in Maine is preparation and training. Depending on where you live, your training will be hard to very difficult as there are not many areas in this country that are as rugged or difficult as the terrain on the AT in Maine. Colorado certainly has higher mountains, and having lived in Boulder, Colorado on and off for several years in my forties and fifties, it took me a while to adjust to living at six thousand feet above sea level. I was in my late sixties before I started hiking the AT.

In my opinion, a gym can help with your upper and lower body strength but I know of nothing that can get you ready for trail hiking other than trail hiking. For any section hiker planning to hike Maine in sections over several years as I did, I had to train each year prior to heading to Maine and as I got older, I had to start earlier with my training as it took more time to get back into shape.

I live in Maryland and unless I wanted to drive ninety-minutes to the AT in Western Maryland or Harpers Ferry, West Virginia to train, I had to settle for local parks in the greater Annapolis and Baltimore area. Patapsco Valley State Park near the Baltimore Washington Thurgood Marshall International Airport, along with the Waterworks Trail and Bacon Ridge Biking Trails, near Annapolis, Maryland, have been my "go to" places to train for these past nine years. The most elevation change I've hiked in any of these local parks is from one-hundred to three-hundred (100-300) feet. In Maine an initial climb can be from one-thousand to three-thousand (1000-3000) feet. Training on local trails does give you a feel for AT hiking, but local trails don't have the large rocks, steep terrain or large roots, but after a good hard rain, you'll get some idea of what it is to hike in mud.

Prior to completing North Carolina in 2016 and Virginia in 2019, I would section hike these states during the months of April and May to get my legs "trail ready". Over the years depending on the number of days we planned to hike in Maine I would start my local training anywhere from four to eight weeks prior to heading north. One of the most critical issues for hiking in Maine is balance and being able to shift weight quickly from one leg to the other. This is a no-brainer for young folks whom I've seen rock hop up or down climbs that I would struggle to climb one or two steps at a time. I've always been amazed and have remarked they remind me of goats the way they quickly flow up and down difficult terrain.

In my opinion, the best months to hike the AT in Maine would be July and August and the early part of September. In May, depending on snow pack, you could have snow to deal with or depending on the spring rain, lots of mud. Beginning in May and for most of June, you also have "black flies" to deal with. Think of "black flies" as horse flies but on steroids. These biting insects have been know to bite through hiking shirts and pants. A long lasting insect prepellant could help, but I've spoken with SoBo Thru Hikers who said even that didn't prevent them from getting bitten.

The other component of training and preparation is having gear that works for you and carrying only what you need along with whatever you need in case of an emergency. This is a good place to discuss backpacking and day hiking, which I call slacking or slackpacking. Backpacking is overnight hiking for one night, multiple nights, or a week or more at a time. Your backpack should have the capacity to carry your sleeping bag or quilt, a pad that goes under your sleeping bag, a tent, and a ground cover to go under your tent. Hammocks have become popular in recent years and if I were starting out I would definitely look into hammocks. Water is critical for hiking and some hikers carry as little as one liter and refill and purify during the day. As an older hiker I prefer to carry at least two and a half liters plus a twelve- or twenty-ounce bottle of Gatorade. I also carry packets of electrolyte powder to add to my water as a backup. Hikers use a number of different ways to purify water and it's wise to purify any water you get from any stream or pond. Water-borne illness can cause cramps, diarrhea and vomiting. There are many ways to purify water. I prefer and use a SteriPen. It uses ultraviolet light to purify a liter of water in about sixty-seconds. One of my hiking partners always carries Acquamira drops to purify his water. Depending on the number of days you will be hiking you will need food for breakfast, lunch, dinner, and for snacks. The weight for this could average between one to two pounds per day. Some hikers don't carry a stove and eat cold and others carry various types of compact stoves to boil water for their meals. Alcohol stoves are very popular and so are Isobutene and propane canisters. I use a Pocket Rocket burner which attaches to a canister in just a few seconds. Jetboil is another commonly used system.

Another critical element for day hiking or backpacking are clothing and footwear. I started out with Merrill trail shoes, then seven-years ago switched to Asolo Boots. As I aged I needed more support and a thicker tread so I wouldn't feel every rock or root underfoot. I suggest that you wait until the end of a day and after you've been on your feet for a long time to get fitted. Your feet will swell the more you are on them and especially if you are carrying a backpack. Having a cramped foot or having your toes constantly hit the front of your footwear will affect any hike you attempt. Good hiking socks are also critical. Again you have many choices but I prefer Darn Tough. Clothing is very personal, but I always carry a rain jacket and a wind shirt.

If I'm backpacking for three-days and two-nights which has been our maximum in Maine, I will wear the same pants, a long sleeve merino wool shirt and a short sleeve running type shirt underneath. I always start out with multiple layers and as the temperature rises and I become warmer, I will shed a layer. Most days I end up hiking in my short sleeve running shirt. I do like a clean and dry pair of socks each day, and I carry two extra pairs in a water-tight zip lock bag. Electrolytes are critical for seniors and I carry two packets for each day. I also carry Jelly-Belly sport beans for an immediate electrolyte boost. I prefer to carry a three-liter Platypus but generally only fill it to either one and a half or two liters, depending on the distance we are hiking that day. In addition I may carry a twelve-ounce Gatorade and a one-liter water bottle that will be about half-full. For a multiday backpack, I prefer having real food for the first day. I've taken lobster rolls, hamburgers, chicken breast, and meatballs that I bought from my previous night's dinner. Cheddar cheese sticks or Babybel cheese are great and depending on the heat can last at least two days.

Most mornings in Maine are cool, even in July and August, temperatures have been in the mid-forties. As I aged, coffee doesn't sit well with me. Now I prefer hot tea in the morning. Using my Pocket Rocket and either my MSR IsoPro fuel canister or Ed's a.k.a. Joker or Jim's a.k.a. Chill, I boil water in my titanium pot and use a collapsible cup for my tea. I hate cleaning pots so I bring paper biodegradable bowls to heat my Organic Ramen Noodles for dinner. They compact down to a two-inch square and go right into my zip lock trash bag. Sometimes

I'll bring hard salami and a few fresh tortillas and that will be my dinner along with a couple of cheese sticks. I used to make instant oatmeal for breakfast and put in a packet of peanut butter or chocolate almond butter. In 2019 on a single overnight hike I just could not tolerate eating oatmeal. I ended up packing out the oatmeal I couldn't eat. Joker suggested belVita breakfast biscuits and I now prefer the blueberry or cinnamon. One or two packets with my hot tea and I'm ready to start my hiking for the day.

Lunches on the first day must be real food and many times I've gotten an extra chicken breast to go or sometimes an extra breakfast sandwich from Dunkin or McDonalds. Organic free range beef jerky and/or Slim Jims work great for a snack or lunch if I combine it with cheese.

I currently have three-ways of carrying my gear depending on whether it's a day hike or a one-night or two-night backpack. For a day hike that involves steep climbs and descents, I prefer my ULA OHM2.0 (ULA Equipment) because of its large deep side pockets. You really don't want your water bottles to slip out of your side pocket half-way into your hike. In parts of the Hundred Mile Wilderness between Johnson Pond Road and north to the gravel road near the south end of Nahmakanta Lake, my Osprey Stratos24 day-pack worked well. I use my older ULA, now called CATALYST for my two-night backpacks as it has firm back support and handles the twenty-four-plus pounds of weight I carry better than my OHM2.0.

I always carry my Garmin inReach Explorer+, a small compass, a three-ounce pocket knife, waterproof matches, first aid stuff including antibiotic cream, either a wool or nylon cap, and an extra pair of reading glasses. I pack my daily meds, ibuprofen, an extra neckerchief, sunglasses, White Mountain Insect Repellant, and extra zip lock bags in a couple of sizes. I carry about thirty (30) feet of light line for hanging my KEVLAR food bag if there are no bear boxes. I always carry a rain jacket on multi-day hikes along with a wind shirt and at times my extremely lightweight REI puffball jacket (Recreational Equipment, Inc.), and fingerless wool gloves that have a mitten cover. I make copies of the pages from AWOL's *AT Guide* for the section or sections we are hiking, along with a small 3x5 inch notepad to record our start and stop times and anything I want to remember. After I finish a hike, I record each days hike in an Excel Spreadsheet I created and write a narrative of the day or days I've hiked in a Word Document. My Excel Spreadsheet has four-hundred-fifteen (415) lines and my Word Document is over four-hundred-fifty (450) pages.

## Actual Training Routines

As I discussed earlier, the difficulty of hiking the various sections in Maine determine when I actually start to train. I usually hike Maine in July and August and unless I have an actual hike planned for June, I will start my training in mid-May. My first training hike is always with my Osprey day-pack and I normally carry about one and one-half liters of water in my Platypus along with a twelve-ounce Gatorade and some light snacks. I normally hike about four miles, two miles in and two miles out and record my time and miles per hour in a notebook I keep in my Subaru Forester.

If the weather is good, I will do the same hike again the next day or maybe add a half mile. I normally take the fourth day off or just walk round my neighborhood. I always wear my boots when I train. After I am comfortable with my progress during the initial training, I add more water and some additional gear like rain jacket, socks, puff ball jacket and increase my miles to three or four miles on my in and out hikes. I always like to take a break on the fourth day. Over the next three to four weeks, I build up to ten to eleven miles a day adding weight until

I'm at my nearly full backpack of twenty-four pounds. Since most of our hikes never exceed ten miles, there isn't a need to train for more than a ten- or eleven-mile-day.

My last training hike with a full pack is normally about two days before I start driving to Maine. I always overnighted someplace in Massachusetts so I have a shorter drive to get to the Hostel the next day. I normally use this day to prepare for the hike which begins the following day.

# Chapter Three

## Hiking Philosophy and Safety

There are some AT Hikers who believe that the AT should only be hiked either always northbound or always southbound. There are others, like me, who believe that one should hike the direction of a particular section based on the terrain. What I mean by this comment is the other seniors that I hike with prefer to hike the steepest terrain early in the day and less steep terrain near the end of the day. This works great for day hikes but will not always work for multi-day and multi-night hikes. Using the Appalachian Trail Conservancy terrain maps, the White Mountains terrain maps, the Guthook app, now FarOut, AWOL's *AT Guide*, other Trail app, sophiaknows.com, and YouTube videos, I've learned to use these tools to determine the best way to hike a particular section or sections.

I've always preferred to use the knowledge and experience of a number of former AT Thru and Section Hikers who have completed the AT either as a Thru Hike or sections over a number of years. Fred F, Ed B, Greg P, Lee and Randy R have been my go-to sources for years. Another factor in our planning is to determine the number of hours it will take us to get to a Lean-to or Shelter if we are hiking for two or three days. We always plan to arrive early so we have a place to sleep in a Lean-to or Shelter.

For example, let's say that the terrain is more favorable if we hike northbound in Maine, but the Shelter we plan to stay is seven-point-five (7.5) miles. For us that is probably an eight- to nine-hour day. If we start at 6:30 A.M., we'd arrive at the Shelter by 4 P.M. at the latest and space would most likely be available. If for some reason we couldn't start until nine, our arrival time at the Shelter would be around 6:30 P.M. or later and we could find the Shelter full.

Even with the excellent information sources, I and my hiking partners spend a considerable amount of time in the planning process and we've changed directions and swapped sections because of weather issues many times. We also prefer to not hike when it's raining as the rocks can be slick and risking a fall at our age is not a great idea. Being above tree line and exposed during a rain storm is a hazard that we always try to avoid.

Day hiking or slacking or slackpacking is normally road to road hiking. I still carry my rain jacket and windshirt, but I only carry food for the day and the amount of water I carry is determined by the distance and how long it will take us to hike that day.

Whether we day hike or backpack, I always make sure my Garmin inReach Explorer+ and cell phone are fully charged and I have a backup charger with me. Jim, a.k.a. Chill always carries the terrain maps for the sections we hike. I carry copies of the pages from AWOL's *AT Guide*, and Ed, a.k.a. Joker carries a compass. I always pack an extra pair of Darn Tough socks along with a space blanket, wool gloves and either my nylon or wool caps. I tend to pack more food than I use hiking in Maine, just in case something happens.

Before we start out each day I use my Garmin inReach Explorer+ to send a pre-formatted text to my family, friends and Jim's wife and at the end of the day I send another that we've finished for the day. If we are running late and we've had a couple of really long, ten- or over eleven-hour-days, I send a specific text to our wives that we are running late so they don't worry.

On one of our Maine hikes, we had to run to a Lean-to and sit out a sudden rain storm for at least an hour and wait for the rain to stop. Normally we would have completed this section by 6 P.M. and Chill's wife would have seen the "Stopping for the day" text. When the text didn't arrive, she called my wife and Madeleine assured her she'd hear from us soon. We didn't finish our hike until 6:45 P.M. on that rain soaked day. Now I send a text message when we are about two miles from our stopping point and if it's after 4 P.M.

I recently read *When You Find My Body* about the disappearance of Geraldine Largay in Maine in July 2013 and the discovery of her remains in October 2015. It reminded me of how important it is to be prepared for any emergency. I personally would never hike Maine solo. I always carry my SteriPen and a set of backup batteries. I almost always have extra food as I don't eat as much as I think I will. I carry an emergency bivy, a wool or nylon cap, wool fingerless glove that have a mitten cover, an extra pair of socks, my REI puffball jacket and a Windshirt. Chill or Joker always carry their Pocket Rocket and a fuel canister and we all carry First aid stuff. For me the most important item is my Garmin inReach Explorer+. I used to carry SPOT GEN3 but I decided to go with Garmin for a number of reasons, one being Garmin has a month to month maintenance plan. I tried carrying a satellite phone once, but it was a lot of weight and I wasn't able to make calls most of the time. Carrying an emergency beacon is critical in Maine, especially for seniors and if you are hiking solo.

# Chapter Four

### New Hampshire US Highway Two to Grafton Notch Maine Highway Twenty-Six (ME 26)

I consider Maine's two-hundred-eighty-one-point-eight (281.8) AT miles (according to AWOL's *2021 AT Guide*) the most demanding, rugged and difficult of all of the fourteen AT states. Having just completed my last ten-point-one (10.1) AT miles in Maine in July 2020, I look at Maine as several different hiking terrains and each has its own degree of difficulty. The GPS coordinates that I have provided are either from AWOL'S *AT Guide* (GPS 44.4010,-71.1094) or from Google Maps or my Garmin inReach Explorer+ (GPS 00.000000,-00.000000). Cell phone service on the AT in Maine is not reliable. Having a GPS device in case of an emergency is critical for this senior and is a wise investment when hiking in Maine and New Hampshire.

### US Highway Two (US 2), Shelburne, New Hampshire to Grafton Notch Maine Highway Twenty-Six (ME 26)

The thirty-one-point-one (31.1) AT miles (*AT Guide to Maine* 15th edition 2009) from US Highway Two (US 2) in Shelburne, New

Hampshire across the New Hampshire/Maine border to Grafton Notch on Maine Highway Twenty-Six (ME 26) does not have a major road crossing. There are a number of access points from both North Road, near Shelburne, New Hampshire and from Success Pond Road, near Berlin, New Hampshire. The sixteen-point-five (16.5) miles of the northern part of New Hampshire AT is somewhat easier than the other AT sections in Maine. I have decided to consider these thirty-one-point-one (31.1) AT miles as a continuous section.

## 2020 – US Highway Two (US 2) Northbound to Gentian Pond Shelter and Campsite and out the Austin Brook Trail, Sunday, July 19th to Monday, July 20th
### Day Eleven and Twelve of Sixteen Days

Starting at US Highway Two (US 2) in Shelburne, New Hampshire there are a couple of access trails to the AT in the sixteen-point-five (16.5) miles before the AT crosses into Maine. We hiked these miles as two separate section hikes.

On our first day, Sunday, July 19th Joker, Chill and I drove up North Road and turned left onto a narrow, pot-holed road. There are a few parking spots where the AT heads northbound. We backpacked north from this parking area, which is about one-point-three (1.3) miles north of US Highway Two (US 2), towards the Trident Col Campsite. The campsite is point-two (.2) miles west of the AT and we tented there on Sunday night. Covid-19 was an issue in 2020 so we tented this year. Joke, Chill and I got negative tests prior to meeting up for our hikes. We had an initial eighteen-hundred-foot (1800) climb over the next three-point-seven (3.7) miles, but none of it was difficult. The campsite had a bear box and we stored our food in it that night. The campsite had a privy too. I recall there were two water sources, with the better one being farther away than the first source. When we hike my cell phone is always on airplane mode so I can take photos. After I had set up my tent, I had the feeling that I needed to turn on my cell and when I did, there was a message from Madeleine. I called and she said that Romeo, our twelve-year-old rescue cat was dying and Cameron and Sheralee would be at Crofton Veterinary Hospital when they put Romeo to sleep. I was shocked and sad and wandered around the tent sites aimlessly. At dusk, I climbed into my tent and cried myself to sleep. A rain storm hit us around midnight and none of us got much sleep that night. On Monday, July 20th, we hiked a very wet trail northbound. We had about a seven-hundred-foot (700) climb over the next two-point-eight (2.8) miles, and again it was not too difficult. We took the turn off to Gentian Pond Shelter and Campsite, hiked point-two (.2) miles east to the shelter. Just beyond the shelter we started down the Austin Brook Trail to my Subaru. The initial part of the Austin Brook Trail was somewhat steep, but the latter part of this trail is pretty flat and exposed to the sun with little or no tree cover. After a long day this was the most uncomfortable part of the hike. There is parking for several cars here (GPS 44.426774,-71.068632) and Millbrook Road connects to North Road and to US Highway Two (US 2).

2019 – 2020 GrandPa Walking one person tent – one pound, one trekking pole

## 2019 – Success Pond Road – Success Trail to AT Southbound to Gentian Pond Shelter and Campsite – Austin Brook Trail, Sunday, August 18th, Day Four of Fourteen Days

Today was a day hike. Success Pond Road can be accessed in Berlin, New Hampshire, off Hutchins Street, and Success Pond Road runs nearly parallel to the AT and northbound to Maine Highway Twenty-Six (ME 26). This road is gravel and has some rough spots.

There are a number of side trails that connect to the AT and I recorded the following GPS Coordinates.

The Success Trail (44.48425,-71.07663) two-point-four (2.4) miles to AT;

Carlo Col Trail, (44.51078,-71.04336) two-point-four (2.4) miles to AT;

Notch Trail (44.53492,-71.02084) two-point-five (2.5) miles to AT;

Speck Pond Trail (44.55961,-71.02280) three-point-six (3.6) miles to AT.

*Source:Appalachian Mountain Club White Mountain Guide, 29th edition, includes pull-out maps*

We hiked in on the Success Trail which was steeper than we expected and took us longer than we had planned. Climbing Mount Success, thirty-five-hundred-sixty-five (3565) feet wasn't hard, but we did have a couple of short and steep climbs and descents to get to the Gentian Pond Shelter and Campsite turnoff. The top of the Austin Brook Trail is a bit steep heading down, but then it's an easy well maintained trail. We hiked three-point-four (3.4) AT and four-point-six (4.6) non-AT miles that day in eight-point-seven-five (8.75) hours. There is parking for several cars here (GPS 44.426774,-71.068632).

## 2019 – Success Pond Road – Notch Trail to AT then Southbound to Success Trail
### Monday, August 26th through Wednesday, August 28th
### Day Twelve through Fourteen of Fourteen Days

This would be a three-day, two Shelter nights hike. We started at 8:36 A.M. We had an easy two-point-five-mile (2.5) hike in from Success Pond Road on the Notch Trail to the AT. We hiked southbound one-point-six (1.6) miles to Full Goose Shelter. The initial eight-hundred-fifty-foot (850) climb up Fulling Mill Mountain South Peak wasn't difficult and the four-hundred-foot (400) climb down to Full Goose Shelter was pretty easy. We got to Full Goose Shelter at 12:30 P.M. It had taken us about four (4) hours to hike three-point-six (3.6) miles. That's a great time for this seventy-eight-year-old hiker. We had followed a young lady in from the parking area and then next saw her and another young man doing maintenance work at Full Goose Shelter.

They were maintaining the privy. The young man, Tigger, had come from Speck Pond Shelter and Campsite earlier that morning and Tigger would be returning later. I was amazed that he would have hiked through Mahoosuc Notch and Arm twice in the same day. I gave them twenty-dollars each and thanked them for their maintenance efforts.

**2019 Monday, August 26th, 12:32 P.M. – Shelter Maintainer's "Tigger" in the middle, GrandPa Walking on right**

Tuesday, August 27th, our second day would be a very difficult day. We started at 7:00 A.M. and we had an initial seven-hundred-foot (700) climb up to Goose Eye Mountain North Peak, then down several hundred feet to Wright Trail by 10:24 A.M. We next hiked three-hundred-thirty (330) feet up to Goose Eye Mountain East Peak. After a snack break, we climbed down to another intersection with Wright Trail again and then back up another two-hundred (200) feet to Goose Eye Mountain West Peak and the Goose Eye Mountain Trail. I lost count of the number of wooden ladders and rebar embedded in the rocks that we climbed and descended that long and difficult day. The final descent down from Goose Eye Mountain West Peak and then the climb up Mount Carlo wore us all out. We reached the turn off to Carlo Col Shelter and Campsite, but still had to hike point-three (.3) miles west to the Shelter. We arrived at the Shelter at 2:25 P.M. Exhausted, I took a nap. These four-point-four (4.4) miles took us nearly seven-point-five (7.5) hours and we were all exhausted. Chill told me I snored loudly during my nap. Normally it's Joker who snores the loudest.

**2019 Tuesday, August 27th, 11:06 A.M. – double set of rebar**

We were up early on Wednesday, August 28th, and left the Shelter to hike our last day in this rugged and difficult section. Before I left Maryland, my friend Ed B. had told me we'd encounter a boulder field after we left Carlo Col Shelter. His boulder field was a steep almost vertical rock wall. I was glad we had started out early today as this would have been much more difficult at the end of the day. Joker with his long legs had no difficulty getting up and through these rocks, but I with my short and older legs had a bit of difficulty. I almost got pushed backwards at one point, but caught myself and got up and through these huge rocks. We had one steeper but a much shorter climb just after crossing the Maine and New Hampshire border. Coming down the Success Trail was hard as my legs were tired from the hard climbs earlier in the day. Our one-point-eight (1.8) AT miles and the two-point-six (2.6) non-AT miles took us five-point-five (5.5) hours. For me this was one of the hardest three days I've ever backpacked.

**2019 Wednesday, August 28th, 7:46 A.M. the wall – hard climb just south of Carlo Col Shelter**

**2019 Wednesday, August 28th, 7:50 A.M. south of Carlo Col Shelter**

## 2017 Success Pond Road, thirteen miles west of Berlin, New Hampshire to Notch Trail to AT Northbound through Mahoosuc Notch, climb Mahoosuc Arm to Speck Pond Shelter and Campsite
## Saturday, July 15th – Sunday, July 16th,
## Day One and Two of Two Days

In July 2017, at the age of seventy-six, I, Chill, Joker and Mello (and his dog Yellow) hiked Mahoosuc Notch and climbed Mahoosuc Arm. I had hired Mello (he worked at Rattle River Lodging & Hostel) to act as our guide as I felt we'd need help getting through what most AT Thru Hikers call "the hardest mile on the AT".

Our original plan was to hike through the Notch, climb the Arm and spend the night at Speck Pond Shelter. On our planned second day, we'd climb Old Speck and descend the twenty-six-hundred (2600) feet over three-point-five (3.5) miles to Grafton Notch on Maine Highway Twenty-six (ME 26) to Chill's rental car.

On Saturday, July 15th around 7:22 A.M., we hiked from the parking area, about point-three (.3) miles off Success Pond Road and two-point-two (2.2) miles to the AT, arriving around 8:40 A.M. (GPS Notch Trail 44.53492,-71.02084) I recall we had some elevation change but it didn't seem a lot. Shortly after we headed north from the south end of Mahoosuc Notch, Mello suggested we put away our trekking poles as they would just be in the way. This was a shock to me as I am totally dependent on my trekking poles especially on rocks. I caused Joker to lose one of his poles in the rocks. The huge boulders and rocks and the surrounding area were wet as Mahoosuc Notch doesn't get a lot of direct sunlight. Think of The Notch as a canyon with steep walls on either side. I lost count on the number of climbs, descents and the times we had to take off our packs to squeeze through the rocks. We had one spot where we had to take off our packs, get on our stomachs and push them ahead of us as we crawled under the rocks. I could feel cold air coming up below me. Mello said that even in the summer there are places that are filled with snow and ice below these rocks. It was cold and damp and the legs of my pants were wet.

**2017 Saturday, July 15th, 9:42 a.m. –
Joker (six-feet-three-inches tall) Mahoosuc Notch**

We had another place where there was a three-foot or more gap between the boulders. I chose not to look down. I passed my pack over to Mello, he then grabbed my left arm and helped pull me across this gap. I doubt if I would have been able to get across without his help.

We reached the north end of Mahoosuc Notch around 12:44 P.M., having hiked one-point-one (1.1) miles in nearly four (4) hours. Actually we had hiked down three-hundred-thirty (330) feet over the last one-point-one (1.1) miles. We took a long and much needed pack off lunch break. We had an excellent water source right at our feet. We drank and then refilled all our water containers.

Over the next five (5) hours, we climbed nearly sixteen-hundred-fifty (1650) feet over one-point-five (1.5) miles. We climbed sheets of solid rock which were still wet in many places. I spent a lot of time crawling on my hands and knees. My pants were wet from the knees down and my knees really hurt. We got to the top of the Arm around 5:50 P.M., and took photos at the top of the Arm.

**2017 Saturday, July 15th, 10:22 A.M.
Mahoosuc Notch "the crawl through"**

2017 Saturday, July 15th, 5:50 P.M. top Mahoosuc Arm
Joker, Chill, GrandPa Walking – photo by Mello

2017 Saturday, July 15th, 5:50 P.M. Top of Mahoosuc Arm
With Joker, GrandPa Walking, Mello and his dog Yellow – Photo by Chill

Over the next hour plus we hiked nearly one more mile over large roots and around Speck Pond to get to Speck Pond Shelter & Campsite. The shelter was brand new having been completed in 2016. We paid our ten dollars per person fee and I paid for Mello's fee. Joker, Chill and I headed for the shelter and Mello said he and Yellow would be tenting.

I was so sore and stiff I could barely climb up and into the shelter. I had ramen for dinner along with some cheese and crackers. I was so exhausted I had to force myself to eat. My knees were raw from the rocks I had crawled up during the day. I didn't sleep well as I had to get up at least three times to pee. Every time I had to get up it was very painful to climb down from the shelter. Even the four ibuprofen I had taken after dinner didn't seem to help my pain.

## 2017 Sunday, July 16th – Speck Pond Shelter & Campsite – Speck Pond Trail to Success Pond Road

I was so sore on Sunday morning that I could hardly get out of the Shelter and I think Joker was hurting too. I had a lot of pain in my left Achilles and I felt I would not be able to make the climb out of Speck Pond and up Old Speck. The twenty-six-hundred-foot (2600) descent over three-point-five (3.5) miles to Grafton Notch and Maine Highway Twenty-six (ME 26) would also be a problem for me, especially with the pain in my left Achilles and the soreness in my knees.

Mello suggested we hike out the three-point-six (3.6) miles on the Speck Pond Trail to Success Pond Road. He said he and Yellow would hike the nearly four miles down Success Pond Road to get my Subaru and bring it to where we'd come out on Success Pond Road. It was a bit after 9 A.M. when we left the Speck Pond Shelter and it was hard for me to climb out from the Shelter. It was even harder for me to hike down the initial steeper part of the Speck Pond Trail as I was in a lot of pain. I had to sit down a number of times as I didn't trust myself hiking down even with my Black Diamond snap-lock trekking poles. I sat down and inched myself down over the wet rocks. As soon as we had hiked down the steeper part of the trail, Mello asked to take off with Yellow and get my Subaru. I agreed and he was out of sight in a matter of minutes. We arrived at Success Pond Road around 2:09 P.M., Mello was there with my Subaru and the AC was running.

I took four more 200mg ibuprofen and drank some Gatorade and drove us to Grafton Notch on Maine Highway Twenty-six (ME 26) so Chill could get his rental. Chill followed me as I drove towards Rattle River Lodging & Hostel. We stopped at Sunday River Brewing Company, Bethel, Maine for a late lunch and I made sure Yellow got lunch too. I paid Mello his fee in cash for the two days he had been our guide. On Monday, July 17th, I drove myself to the Emergency Room in Berlin and the doctor confirmed that I had injured my left Achilles. This would end my July 2017 hiking in Maine and New Hampshire. Joker and Chill would head to Vermont the next day to hike several days before heading home and I would head home on Tuesday, July 18th. I would return to Maine in August 2017 and section hike more of Maine's AT.

### 2018 Sunday, August 19th, Speck Pond Shelter & Campsite
### Monday, August 20th, Grafton Notch,
### Maine Twenty-Six (ME 26), nineteen miles west of Andover
### Day Seven and Eight of Twelve Days

It would be another year before Joker, Chill and I would complete these last miles of the AT between Shelburne, New Hamphire US Highway Two (US 2) and Grafton Notch and Maine Highway Twenty-six (ME 26). We decided to get a shuttle drop to Success Pond Road and the Speck Pond Trail instead of leaving a car that we would have to drive back to. Paul Dom decided to hike with us and that reduced our cost to thirty-dollars a person. We always paid cash for our shuttles. We started hiking around 7:24 A.M. and the first mile or so was very easy, but the wet grass soaked my hiking pants and boots. We had a few short and steep climbs and arrived at Speck Pond Shelter & Campsite around 11:24 A.M. This hike was much easier than it was in July 2017. We ate lunch and I had the rest of the day to rest. The caretaker asked us not to cook in the shelter but I had already made dinner. Chill, Joker and Paul had to use the cooking area nearby. Paul tented in his ultra-light tent that night.

On Monday morning July 20th we were all up by 6:00 A.M. but it was dark and cold in the shelter as the sun rose from behind the shelter. I put on my gloves and puff ball jacket to keep warm. We finished breakfast and left around 7:17 A.M. We had an initial very hard and steep six-hundred-forty-foot (640) climb over one-point-one (1.1) miles out of Speck Pond Shelter & Campsite. The first part of the climb was like a narrow chimney and we stopped a lot to rest. The caretaker climbs this twice a day to get instructions and a weather report. She's one tough lady.

**AT Passport Stamp – 2017 Wednesday, August 23rd**

The Appalachian Trail Passport book has been around since 2013. Most Thru Hikers and many Section Hikers purchase the AT Passport and get it stamped at Hostels, Restaurants, Hotels, Motels, Shuttles, AMC Huts, and other businesses along the AT.

**2018 Monday, August 20th, 8:53 A.M. Climbing Old Speck (highest point in Southern Maine) – photo by Chill**

We arrived at the turn off to the summit at 9:25 A.M. but decided not to hike the point-three (.3) miles to the summit and started our long twenty-six-hundred-foot (2600) descent over the next three-point-five

(3.5) miles to Grafton Notch. I lost count on the number of times I had to stop, sit and rest my legs. Even though I wore my Copper Fit soft knee braces my knees burned and ached. We were back at my Subaru Forester by 2:21 P.M. Paul sent us the photos he had taken, but our emails to contact him about hiking with us again went unanswered.

Summary
July 2020 two-days, one tent night;
August 2019 one day hike; three-days, two shelter nights;
July 2017 two-days, one Shelter night;
August 2018 two-days, one Shelter night

We hiked these thirty-one-point-one (31.1) AT miles and seventeen-point-nine (17.9) access non-AT trail miles between US Highway Two (US 2) in Shelburne, New Hampshire and Grafton Notch Maine Highway Twenty-Six (ME 26) as five separate hiking trips and ten days of hiking. We averaged four-point-nine (4.9) miles per day.

## Chapter Five
### Grafton Notch Maine Highway Twenty-Six (ME 26), Nineteen Miles West of Andover, Maine – Northbound to East Flagstaff Road

East Flagstaff Road is at the north end of the Bigelow State Preserve and one-hundred-seventy-one (171) miles from Katahdin. This section is by far the most rugged and difficult part of Maine's AT and for the three of us it was a challenge every time we hiked these ninety-six (96) tough, rugged and steep AT miles. There wasn't anything easy about these next AT miles. I always made sure my Garmin inReach Explorer+ was charged, Chill always had the terrain maps and the three of us always made sure we had our water purifiers with us and an extra fuel canister. I always packed a space blanket and an extra pair of socks, even when we slacked. In addition I always packed a pair of gloves and either my nylon or wool cap. I always carry both matches and a propane lighter.

## 2018 Grafton Notch, Maine Highway Twenty-Six (ME 26), Northbound to East B Hill Road, eight miles east of Andover, Maine
### Sunday, July 15th through Tuesday, July 17th – Three-day two-night backpack
### Day Seven through Day Nine of Twelve Days

On Sunday, July 15th, 2018 around 8:24 A.M. we hiked north from Grafton Notch. We had an almost immediate continuous steep and tough climb up grades greater than fifteen to twenty percent (15-20%) to Baldpate Lean-to. It took us nearly two-point-five (2.5) hours to climb twelve-hundred (1200) feet over two-point-three (2.3) miles. Looking back this was actually pretty good time. We considered hiking the next three-point-five (3.5) miles to the next Lean-to but the forecast called for rain and getting caught on the exposed and above tree line Baldpate West or East Peak in the rain would have been dangerous. The rain hit about an hour after we got to the Lean-to. We stayed dry that day and we were all happy we had made the correct decision to stay at Baldpate Lean-to.

On Monday, July 16th we left Baldpate Lean-to around 7:25 A.M. and it was very cool that day, almost cold. We immediately had a very steep one-thousand-foot (1000) climb up Baldpate West peak, followed by a steep drop of probably four- to five-hundred (400-500) feet. The climb up Baldpate East peak was shorter but much steeper than Baldpate West. From Baldpate East Peak at thirty-eight hundred-ten (3810) feet we had an almost continuous steep drop of fifteen-hundred (1500) feet over one-point-eight (1.8) miles to Frye Notch Lean-to. We arrived around 2 P.M. It had taken us a little over six (6) hours to hike three-point-five (3.5) miles. Joker, Chill and I shared the Lean-to with a southbound Thru Hiker (SoBo) who offered me weed to smoke. Yes, and I enjoyed a couple of hits. Chill recalled that I offered a supposed "hard luck hiker" twenty dollars only to find out later from Yukon, the owner of Human Nature Hostel, that this "hard luck hiker" had been conning other hikers on the trail. He was questioned in Gorham, New Hampshire by the police about a week later after a hiker complained that money was missing from her tent site.

On Tuesday, July 17th we left Frye Notch Lean-to around 6:48 A.M. with our rain pack covers on as it felt like rain. We had an easier five-hundred-foot (500) climb which was considerably easier than any climb over the previous two days. Over the next three-point-eight (3.8) miles we descended one-thousand (1000) feet and stopped briefly at Dunn Notch and Falls around 10:25 A.M. for a much needed pack off and snack break. We arrived at East B Hill Road around 11:19 A.M. (GPS 44.668438,-70.893179), and spent Tuesday night, July 17th at Human Nature Hostel near Andover.

**2018 Monday, July 16th, 11:27 A.M. – GrandPa Walking using rope to climb down to wood ladder – photo by Chill**

The Hostel was open in 2017, but not listed in AWOL's *AT Guide* until 2018. We had three-beds on the upper level of the Geodesic dome structure. Wednesday, July 18th was our first Zero Day and I went back to bed after breakfast and slept for several hours. I've never done that before.

**2018 Monday, July 16th, 10:03 A.M. Baldpate West Peak – Joker leading, GrandPa Walking next – photo by Chill**

**2018 South Arm Road, nine miles east of Andover, Southbound to East B Hill Road, eight miles east of Andover**
**Thursday, July 19th – Friday, July 20th –**
**Two-day one night backpack**
**Days Eleven and Twelve of Twelve Days**

We decided to hike southbound from South Arm Road to East B Hill Road because my friend Fred F said the climbs would be steeper and the descents somewhat less steep. We headed southbound from South

Arm Road (GPS 44.721359,-70.786007) on Thursday, July 19th at 7:58 A.M. It was cold that morning and I was still chilled and hadn't been able to get warm yet. We had a stream to cross that would require rock hopping. As I watched Joker cross the stream I noticed a larger than normal step down from one rock to another and I felt that with my full pack this step down would be a problem for me. I asked Chill to carry my pack so I could rock hop without any weight on my back. He carried his pack across, came back and took my lighter pack and rock hopped for the third time. I started to cross and being chilled I took my time. I had to sit down on one rock so I didn't have to make a large step down and this worked great for me. Once on the other side we had a thousand-foot (1000) climb over the next one-point-eight (1.8) miles to Moody Mountain. At times the grade was greater than twenty-five-percent (25%). I warmed up quickly during the thousand-foot, very steep at times climb. From Moody Mountain we climbed down nearly fourteen-hundred (1400) feet to Sawyer Brook campsite and crossed over Sawyer Road shortly thereafter. We had several streams to cross and then a sixteen-hundred-foot (1600) steep climb over one-point-four (1.4) miles. We got to Hall Mountain Lean-to just after 1:40 P.M. It had taken us about six (6) hours to cover four-point-one (4.1) miles.

**2018 Thursday, July 19th 10:30 A.M. –
climb down rebar – photo by Chill**

We were all up Friday at 6 A.M. and by 6:45 A.M. we were heading southbound. We had an easy and not too steep climb of three-hundred (300) feet to Wyman Mountain and a long and gradual drop of fourteen-hundred-fifty (1450) feet over the next four-point-seven (4.7) miles. We stopped a number of times to rest our sore and aching knees. We were back at my Subaru by 11:15 A.M. We had hiked these six (6) miles in just under five-point-five (5.5) hours. This was excellent time for this terrain. We headed back to Human Nature Hostel. Chill looked at the forecast and it showed rain in the forecast for Sunday through Tuesday. We agreed to head home the next day rather than wait out the rain over the next four days. We'd come back to Maine in August 2018 to hike more Maine AT miles.

## 2020 Dirt Road (South of Maine Highway Seventeen ME 17) Southbound to Bemis Mountain Lean-to and southbound to South Arm Road
### Thursday, July 9th and Friday, July 10th – two-day one night backpack
### Days One and Two of Sixteen Days

This would be the first of my last two AT sections I'd hike to complete Maine's AT in 2020. Chill still has parts of the Hundred Mile Wilderness and Joker still has Katahdin to climb. We had hiked the one mile from the Dirt Road north to Maine Highway Seventeen on a Nero Day in 2019 as we wanted to eliminate the extra mile in this tough section. A Nero Day is a day when you hike only a few miles. A Zero Day is a no hike day and a day to rest.

Covid-19 was a concern of ours and we had arranged to have "Honey" at The Cabin make dinner for us that Friday evening after we finished our two-day backpack. We had originally planned to slack pack from Bald Mountain Road (south of Monson) to Moxie Pond but Chill looked at the weather and we all agreed that we should backpack this section first.

We started south from the Dirt Road at 7:46 A.M. (GPS 44.8347,-70.7242) with an initial very steep climb of fourteen-hundred (1400) feet over the next two-point-two (2.2) miles to Bemis Mountain Second Peak. Once we topped Bemis Mountain Second Peak it was an easy hike to Bemis Mountain Lean-to. We encountered several blow downs where fallen trees had blocked the AT. This is pretty common in Maine as the remoteness of the AT makes clearing blow downs difficult. We arrived around 12:10 P.M., having hiked the three-point-five (3.5) miles in about four-point-five (4.5) hours. Part of our original plan was to hike to the Bemis Stream Trail and stealth tenting. I researched the area but I could not find any water sources nearby and we didn't want to take a chance of trying to find three tent sites and not have access to water.

**2020 Thursday, July 9th, 9:42 A.M. –
Chill climbing over one of many blow downs**

We were all up as soon as it was light on Friday, July 10th and we started our climb up Bemis Mountain. We had a five-hundred-foot (500) climb over the next one-point-seven (1.7) miles and it was a lot easier than our climb yesterday. When we got to the Bemis Stream Trail, Chill saw that there were at least three places to tent, but no water source. We had made the better choice to stay at Bemis Mountain Lean-to yesterday.

There was a stream about point-three (.3) miles further south, but I can't remember if there was much of a flow. We stopped at a real man-made bench at 11:10 A.M. and snacked on a pack off break. The six-hundred-foot (600) climb up Old Blue was steep in part but not difficult. I'm not sure if I would have wanted to hike this northbound. It was almost 2:45 P.M. and we still had a very long twenty-two-hundred-foot (2200) descent ahead of us. The hike down was really hard on my knees, and I stopped a lot to rest. The final descent of eight-hundred (800) feet over the last half-mile was the worst part of today's hike. There were a couple of iron railings in the rocks and rock steps to help, but it was a constant steep down all the way to South Arm Road. We arrived at my Subaru at 6:55 P.M. It had taken us nearly thirteen (13) hours to hike eight-point-seven (8.7) miles. We were all exhausted.

**2020 Friday, July 10th, 6:37 P.M. rebar Yup, it's that steep**

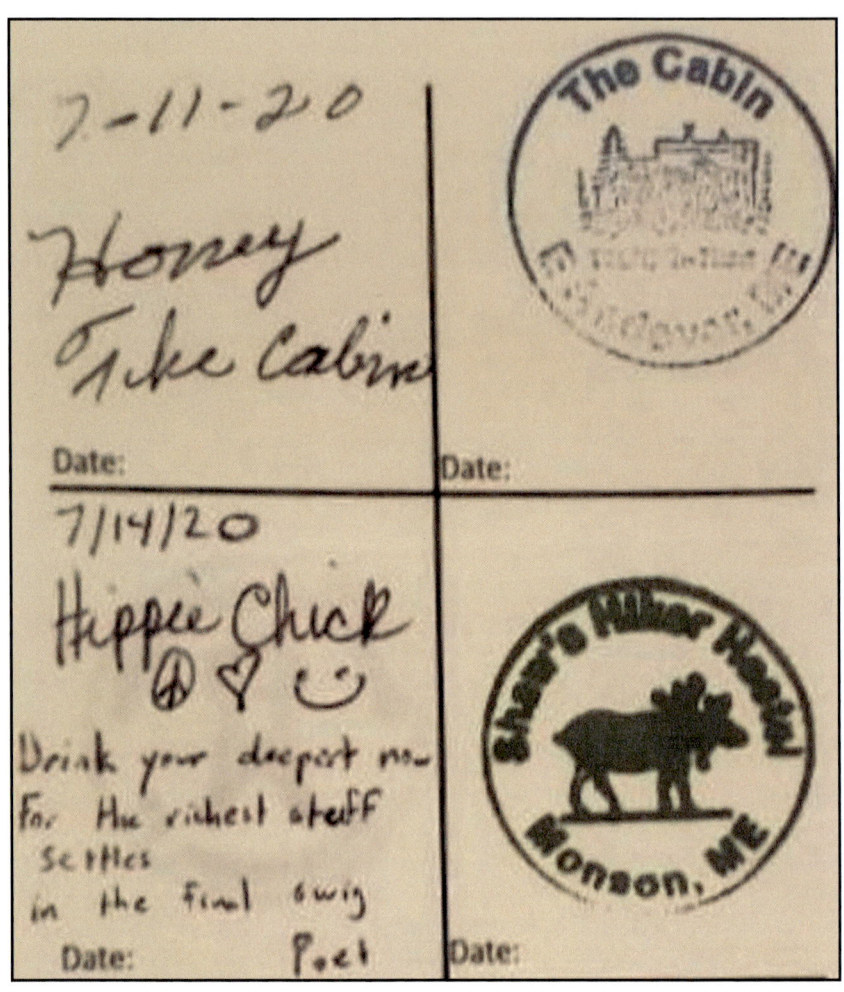

**2020 July The Cabin and Shaw's Hiker Hostel – Maine**

    I tried calling "Honey" at the Cabin several times and kept getting a busy signal. I didn't have her cell so I couldn't text her with my Garmin inReach either. We arrived at the Cabin around 7:30 P.M. and "Honey" came out to greet us. She and her husband "Bear" (deceased) are the "Legends" on the AT. Honey told us she wasn't sure we were coming as an electrical storm had knocked out their landline. That's why I couldn't reach her. She was glad we had arrived safely. We washed up and sat down to a lasagna dinner. I ate a lot more than I normally do at this late hour, but I was really hungry tonight. "Honey" also made strawberry shortcake and I had a small piece.

After dinner, Joker got the single room, and Chill and I shared a room that "Honey" had never rented before. It had an AC unit that was noisy, but it didn't keep me up. I was out like a light tonight. I didn't even wake up during the night to use the bathroom. "Honey" and her young friend made breakfast for us. I ate a lot more than I normally do but I was extremely hungry this morning. We paid our bills in cash as we knew this would help out "Honey". We headed back to the Dirt Road to pick up Joker's truck and Chill's rental and drove to Monson where I would hike my last ten-point-one (10.1) miles of Maine's two-hundred-eighty-one-point-eight (281.8) (AWOL's *2020 AT Guide*) AT miles.

## 2018 Maine Highway Seventeen (ME 17), eleven miles west of Oquossoc Northbound to Maine Highway Four (ME 4), nine miles west of Rangeley
## Monday, August 13th – Tuesday, August 14th –
## Two-day one night backpack
## Days One and Two of Twelve Days

It has always been part of our planning to try and hike an easier day or two when we hike in Maine and I thought this would be a good start for our August hikes this year.

We started northbound from the parking area (GPS 44.8364,-70.7100) on Maine Highway Seventeen (ME 17) at 7:18 A.M. and had a rather easy climb of one-hundred-fifty (150) feet over the next three-point-eight (3.8) miles. There were a lot of bog boards, some in great shape and others not so great. We also had a few steep but short climbs. We arrived at Sabbath Day Pond Lean-to at 10:34 A.M., having covered the three-point-eight (3.8) miles in about three-point-five (3.5) hours.

A one-mile-per-hour pace is great for us seniors in Maine. Normally we have a Lean-to ourselves or maybe with one or two others. That night the Lean-to was full and we were packed in like I experienced in the Smokies.

We were up early on Tuesday and we had some light rain. We left at 7:07 A.M. in a light rain and hiked up about one-point-six (1.6) miles to a powerline. It was one of the first I've seen in Maine. The trail was very wet and muddy so we had to slow down a lot.

We finished in the rain at 3:24 P.M., having covered the nine-point-four (9.4) miles in just under nine (9) hours. Again our one-mile-per-hour was a great pace for us today.

**AT Passport Stamp – closed in 2019**

2018 Tuesday, August 14th, 12:33 P.M. Maine mud

### 2018 Saddleback Mountain Southbound to Maine Highway Four (ME 4), nine miles west of Rangeley
### Friday, July 13th – one day hike
### Day Five of Twelve Days

When we first started to plan our hikes between Maine Highway Four (ME 4) near Rangeley and Maine Highway Twenty-Seven (ME 27) near Stratton, I started to look at ways we could break up this thirty-two-point-two-mile (32.2) difficult section into several shorter hikes. We'd been told about the old ski trail up Saddleback Mountain and decided we could use the ski trail to day hike this section.

We started hiking up from the base of the closed Saddleback Ski Lodge (GPS 44.946282,-70.527600) at 7:23 A.M. and hiked up a mostly dirt and gravel trail about one-point-eight (1.8) miles to Saddleback Mountain at forty-one-hundred-twenty (4120) feet, arriving at 9:24 A.M. (GPS 44.934770,-70.506995). The grade was pretty constant and mostly a continuous climb. There were few level spots to rest. We then headed southbound and down fifteen-hundred (1500) feet over the next two-point-one (2.1) miles. The trail was steep in part but not too difficult. We didn't stop at Plazza Rock Lean-to and continued down to Maine Highway Four (ME 4). We got to my Subaru at 3:55 P.M. (GPS 44.8869,-70.5405). It had taken us eight-point-five (8.5) hours to hike five-point-seven (5.7) miles. We ate at Forks in the Air that night in Rangeley. This restaurant has the best food in Rangeley and is pricey, but worth the cost.

2018 Friday, July 13th – 1 P.M. climbing down from
Saddleback Mountain – photo by Chill

## 2019 Barnjum Road Southbound to Saddleback Mountain
### Thursday, July 18th – Friday, July 19th –
### Two day one night backpack
### Days Eleven and Twelve of Seventeen Days

We'd been told about Barnjum Road as an access point to the AT by the Owners of Fieldstone Cottages in Rangeley. AWOL's *AT Guide* calls it "Barnjam Rd" but the road sign is Barnjum Road. From Rangeley drive south on Maine Highway Four (ME 4) about twenty-one (21) miles to Maine Highway One-Forty-Two (ME 142). Turn left onto

Maine Highway One-Forty-Two (ME 142) and drive about two-point-five (2.5) miles to East Madrid Road. Turn left onto East Madrid Road and drive about five-point-two (5.2) miles to Barnjum Road. It's a sharp right turn onto Barnjum Road, and it's about two-point-two (2.2) miles on a gravel road to the first bridge. Bear left after the bridge and continue about point-five (.5) miles to next bridge. Again bear left after the bridge and cross the third bridge about point-three (.3) miles later. Continue on road until you see several large boulders on your left. The gravel road continues to the right.

There is parking here for a couple of cars. (GPS 44.955674,-70.370522) We started hiking on what was an old road now filled with tall wet grass at 7:10 A.M. We got to the AT around 7:52 A.M. and headed southbound. The trail drops about seven-hundred (700) feet over the next one-point-four (1.4) miles and we had a short walk on Woods Road.

In July 2013, Geraldine Largay disappeared somewhere south of Woods Road and north of Oberton Stream. Her remains were found on October 14, 2015 about one-thousand (1000) yards north of the AT and near two streams in very dense woods. If only her husband had known about access to the AT from Barnjum Road maybe Gerry would have survived.

We rock hopped Oberton Stream as the water level was low this July in 2019. We had a series of steep climbs of fourteen-hundred (1400) feet over the next two-point-seven (2.7) miles to Popular Ridge Lean-to. We arrived just after 1 P.M. and after putting my boots and socks out to dry I laid down for a nap.

**2019 Thursday, July 18th, 9:45 A.M. – Joker and GrandPa Walking rock hopping Oberton Stream – photo by Chill**

On Wednesday night, July 17th, 2019, after we finished dinner, I stopped at Pine Tree Frosty in Rangeley to get a lobster roll to go. I asked them to double wrap it in aluminum foil and I put in the mini-fridge we had at Cottage Five of the Fieldstone Cottages. I ate my lobster roll at Popular Ridge Lean-to for dinner that Thursday, along with a package of cheese and crackers and a package of mixed fruit and nuts. I love to have fresh food for my first night of backpacking.

 We slept in on Friday until 6:50 A.M. and by 8:18 A.M. we were heading southbound. We had a steep, very hard seven-hundred-foot (700) climb up Saddleback Junior. We also had steep descents down from Saddleback Junior and then a steeper eight-hundred-fifty-foot (850) climb up The Horn. It was another steep descent from The Horn and steep but short climb up to the first part of Saddleback Mountain. We had an easy but long walk across the exposed above tree-line ridge of Saddleback Mountain to the trail down to the Ski Lodge. (GPS 44.934770,-70.506995) It was 3:30 P.M. and it had taken us almost eight (8) hours to hike five (5) miles. The gravel trail down to the closed Ski Lodge seemed steeper today. It was also very hot and there was no breeze after we descended below the summit. I slipped and landed on my left elbow and got several cuts and scrapes. I applied my antibiotic after cleaning the wound and applied a bandage. It was nearly 5:30 P.M. by the time we got back to my Subaru. I had reserved a Lake Cabin at Town & Lake Motel and Joker took one room. Chill and I shared the other. It wasn't air conditioned but the ceiling fans worked great.

**2019 Lobster Roll – Popular Ridge Lean-to**
**Thursday evening, July 18th**

**2019 Friday, July 19th, 11:06 A.M. GrandPa
Walking climbing The Horn – photo by Chill**

## 2018 Caribou Valley Road Southbound to Barnjum Road
## Monday, July 9th – Tuesday, July 10th –
## two day one night backpack
## Days One and Two of Twelve Days

We arranged a shuttle drop, but looking back my Subaru Forester could have easily handled this very rough pot-holed road. (GPS 45.045886,-70.346163) We started at 8 A.M. and walked the half-mile past the barricade to the AT. We started hiking southbound at 8:38 A.M. and had a very steep climb of fourteen-hundred (1400) feet to Sugarloaf Mountain over the next two-point-one (2.1) miles. At times the grade was nearly thirty-five-percent (35%). We had another short and very steep climb up Spaulding Mountain, followed by a seven-hundred-foot (700) descent that was very steep (sit down and slide steep) at times to Spaulding Mountain Lean-to. We had hiked the five-point-two (5.2) miles in just under seven-point-five (7.5) hours. Today was a long and hard hiking day for us.

On Tuesday, July 10th, we left the Spaulding Mountain Lean-to at 7:24 A.M. Chill and I thought Joker had taken a wrong turn and we waited and then Chill went back to check. Joker was ahead of us the entire time. When starting out for the day it's important for all hiking partners to be in view of each other initially. This is critically important in Maine.

After reaching Lone Mountain the trail descended one-thousand (1000) feet to Barnjum Road and it was steep in part but overall a great trail. We reached the junction of the AT and Barnjum Road at 11:17 A.M. and we had a short walk in a hot cloudless day back to my Subaru, arriving at 11:59 A.M. We had hiked three-point-nine (3.9) miles in just under four (4) hours. I unlocked the car doors and started the engine. As I was walking around the hood, a snake came out from under the hood. Scared the crap out of me. I carefully opened the hood to make sure it was alone. This was my second snake on the AT. My first was in Virginia and was a copperhead!

2018 Tuesday, July 10th – Snake under Subaru Hood – Photo by Chill

## 2018 Caribou Valley Road Northbound to Maine Highway Twenty-Seven (ME 27), Stratton
### Wednesday, July 11th – one day hike
### Day Three of Twelve Days

We decided to drive ourselves back to Caribou Valley Road today and started at 7:02 A.M. We climbed about six-hundred (600) feet over one-point-one (1.1) miles to Crocker Cirque Campsite turn off. It took us just under an hour today. Over the next one-point-one (1.1) miles we had a number of very steep climbs up thirteen-hundred (1300) feet to South Crocker Mountain. We peaked around 9:56 A.M. We then hiked down then back up North Crocker, about one mile, arriving at the peak at 11:12 A.M. We descended twenty-nine-hundred (2900) feet over the next five-point-two (5.2) miles. My knees ached a lot and we stopped a lot to rest. I was glad we were hiking with daypacks as my backpack weight would have been a lot harder on my knees.

2018 Wednesday, July 11th, 9 A.M. – Joker and GrandPa Walking South Crocker Mountain – photo by Chill

**2019 Maine Highway Twenty-Seven (ME 27)**
**Northbound to East Flagstaff Road**
**Monday, July 8th – Wednesday, July 10th –**
**three days, two night backpack**
**Days One through Three of Seventeen Days**

I spent a lot of time speaking with Fred F, Randy, Ed B and others about this section of the AT. They all agreed that these would be our hardest days yet. The original plan was to hike these sixteen-point-seven (16.7) miles over four days.

We started at 7:34 A.M. (GPS 45.1034,-70.3569) at Maine Highway Twenty-Seven (ME 27) and the trail to the Cranberry Stream Campsite was rather easy for Maine. Over the next nearly three (3) miles we climbed two-thousand (2000) feet and experienced some of the steepest and hardest climbs of my AT experience. We were carrying full packs and four days of food. My pack was about twenty-four (24) pounds. We passed the Bigelow Range Trail at 11:05 A.M. and arrived at Horn Pond Lean-to just after 2:14 P.M. It had taken us six-point-five (6.5) hours to hike five-point-one (5.1) miles. My left Achilles started to hurt almost as soon as we started climbing today. I took four ibuprofen as soon as we got to the Lean-to and four more again just before climbing into my Big Agnes down sleeping bag that night. I also applied Arnica to both my Achilles and aching knees.

**2019 Monday, July 8th, 12:56 P.M. – GrandPa Walking climb up to Horns Pond Lean-to – photo by Chill**

On Tuesday, July 9th, I took four more ibuprofen with my breakfast and my left Achilles didn't hurt as much as it did on Monday. We started at 6:34 A.M. and had another steep climb up South Horn followed by a steep down of several hundred feet. We had another very steep seven-hundred-foot (700) climb up Bigelow Mountain West Peak (4145 feet). We hiked down several hundred feet on a very steep trail to the turn off to Avery Memorial Campsite, which was another point-two (.2) miles off the AT. It was nearly 10:25 A.M. when we arrived. This was supposed to be our second night but the water source here wasn't great and we all agreed to hike the additional two-point-four (2.4) miles to the turn off to Safford Notch Campsite and the additional point-three (.3) miles to the tent site.

**2019 Tuesday, July 9th, 10:25 A.M. – Avery Peak GrandPa Walking – photo by Chill**

The hike up Avery Peak was totally exposed, above the tree line, and rocky. I chose not to look down and kept my eyes always looking forward or up. I was very tired as my left Achilles was hurting again. It was very windy on this difficult climb and we all decided not to take a break but hike on and get out of the wind. Over the next nearly eighteen-hundred (1800) feet and two (2) miles, we had a number of steep descents from Avery Peak to the turn off to Safford Notch Campsite. I was totally exhausted by the time we got to the campsite and I took the first level tent spot I found. I set up my one-pound tent that I had bought from Fred F earlier this year. I sort of got it right, but I was just too tired to do anything more. I ate something but I wasn't really hungry and I knew I was overtired and exhausted. We had hiked five-point-three (5.3) AT miles and another point-seven (.7) miles in just over nine-point-five (9.5) hours and had combined our planned two days of hiking into a single hiking day. I can't remember if I got up to pee that night.

On Wednesday morning July 10th, we left Safford Notch Campsite and hiked the point-three (.3) miles to the AT and then headed north. The walk out to the AT today seemed a lot easier today than yesterday. Over the next three-point-two (3.2) miles, we climbed seven-hundred-fifty (750) feet to Little Bigelow Mountain and today's terrain was a lot easier than yesterday by a huge factor. I had taken four ibuprofen before we started but my left Achilles still hurt. We reached Bigelow Mountain around 10 A.M. and we determined we still had three-point-one (3.1) miles to hike and a descent of eighteen-hundred (1800) feet. We finished just after 3 P.M. having covered six-point-three (6.3) miles in just under eight (8) hours.

These past three days were extremely difficult and exhausting and I had some degree of pain in my left Achilles most of the time. At times it was just putting one boot in front of the other and looking forward to the next sit down and rest stop. I was looking forward to the next two Zero Days to rest, relax and do absolutely nothing.

## Summary

July 2018 three days, two Lean-to nights; two days, one Lean-to night;

July 2020 two days, one Lean-to night;

August 2018 two days, one Lean-to night;

July 2018 one day hike;

July 2019 two days, one Lean-to night;

July 2018 two days, one Lean-to night; one day hike

July 2019 three days, one Lean-to, one tent night.

We hiked nine separate hikes, hiked ninety-six (96) AT and seven-point-six (7.6) non-AT miles over eighteen (18) days. We averaged five-point-eight (5.8) miles per day.

# Chapter Six
## East Flagstaff Road to Main Highway Fifteen (ME 15) Three-point-six (3.6) miles east off Monson Maine

The next fifty-seven (57) miles from East Flagstaff Road, across the Kennebec River and northbound to Monson are some of the easier miles in Maine. Again, there is nothing easy about hiking the AT in Maine, but these miles lack the climbs and descents of the previous sections south of East Flagstaff Road.

**East Flagstaff Road to Kennebec River**
**2019 Scott Road Southbound to East Flagstaff Road**
**Saturday, July 13th – Sunday, July 14th –**
**Two days, one Lean-to night**
**Days Six and Seven of Seventeen Days**

Leaving a vehicle at East Flagstaff Road is easy because AWOL's *2020 AT Guide* provides GPS coordinates (GPS 45.1346,-70.1714). Getting to Scott Road was not easy, and we had two choices. The first choice is to follow the Google Map GPS directions and drive ten miles on very narrow and at times less than one and a half car width rutted and rough roads to Scott Road. The second choice was to drive much better roads, but drive nearly sixty (60) miles, taking at least nearly two hours. Chill and I drove it both ways and we decided the longer drive via Bingham, Maine was better. My Subaru Forester handled the rough and pot-holed roads better than Chill's rental.

There is no parking on Scott Road but I was able to park on the shoulder of a side road near the AT (GPS 45.203172,-70.074255). Joker helped me to back in so I was off Scott Road and I didn't block travel on the side road. We started south around 8:26 A.M. with a swarm of Maine gnats to fight off. The next five-point-seven (5.7) miles took us three-point-five (3.5) hours and we had several ups and downs with few rocky parts and the roots we encountered were a lot smaller in this part of Maine. This was some of the easiest terrain in Maine. AWOL doesn't show much elevation change but the Maine terrain map five shows several hundred feet of ups and downs. Chill always carries a terrain map and he also uses the Guthook app (now called FarOut) on his smartphone.

**2019 Saturday, July 13th, 9:18 A.M. GrandPa Walking and Joker Boards around West Carry Pond – Photo by Chill**

We arrived at West Carry Pond Lean-to just after noon. We had the Lean-to to ourselves until around five in the afternoon when other hikers arrived. We had a visit in the early afternoon from an older man who lived on the other side of West Carry Pond. We also had a visit from a couple and their two young children around 5 P.M. They brought hot dogs to grill and lemonade for us hikers. This was my first "Trail Magic" in Maine. I love hot dogs and even after eating an early dinner I couldn't resist. Trail Magic is when someone shows up at a Shelter, Lean-to, or road crossing with real food and cold drinks.

**2019 Saturday, July 13th, 5:30 P.M. – Family brought hot dogs and lemonade to West Carry Pond Lean-to "First Maine Trail Magic"**

We were up around 5:30 A.M. on Sunday, July 14th, but didn't leave the Lean-to until 8:20 A.M. I didn't sleep much last night as I had to get up at least four times to pee. It felt very humid today and it felt like it would rain at any time. The terrain today had a few more ups and downs and one very short climb, but we covered the six-point-three (6.3) miles in about five (5) hours. I rode with Chill, and Joker followed us in his truck to the Caratunk House in Caratunk, Maine, on the north side of the Kennebec River. We spent the night at The Caratunk House Bed & Breakfast Hostel run by Paul Fuller. I had a private room at the top of a steep set of stairs and Joker and Chill shared a room on the other side of the stairs. There was a common bathroom next to my room. Joker used the bathroom at least once that night.

## 2019 Caratunk, across the Kennebec River South to Scott Road
## Monday, July 15th – One day hike
## Day Eight of Seventeen Days

Breakfast at The Caratunk House was great that morning and very filling. Only Shaw's in Monson and Mountain Harbour B&B & Hostel on US 19E in North Carolina are better. The free canoe shuttle starts around 9 A.M. but we wanted to get an earlier start and Paul suggested Cheryl Anderson. It was worth the extra dollars to be paddled across the Kennebec River at 8 A.M. We started from the south side of the Kennebec River around 8:25 A.M. and had a short and steep climb initially then a more gradual climb over the three miles to Otter Pond Road. We've heard good things about Harrison's Pierce Pond Camps from both Paul in Caratunk and other hikers. It was 11:21 A.M. when we passed Piece Pond Lean-to. I was having a lot of pain in my right heel, but I said nothing to Joker or Chill and we continued to hike south. We got back to my Subaru just after 2:17 P.M., having covered the eight-point-three (8.3) miles in just over six (6) hours. It was a very long drive to Caratunk, Maine to get Chill's rental and Joker's truck and a much longer drive to Rangeley. I didn't care as we would have the next two Zero Days off before our next hike.

2019 Monday, July 22nd, 12:16 P.M.
Volunteer transports hikers across Kennebec River

**2019 Monday, July 15th, 8:17 A.M. Crossing Kennebec River
Cheryl with Paddle**

## 2019 Boise-Cascade Logging Road
## Southbound to Kennebec River
## Monday, July 22nd – One Day Hike
## Day Fifteen of Seventeen Days

This would be our last two days of section hiking in Maine this July in 2019 as I was very tired and if we hiked anywhere else it would have to be a lot easier. After another great breakfast at The Caratunk House, we got another shuttle to our start point which we found out from Paul was not the Logging Road but a side road a few hundred feet further north of the Logging Road. We started at 8:33 A.M. and had a very easy and mostly descending hike on a very easy trail (for Maine) to the Kennebec River. We stopped and visited with the young man who provides the canoe shuttles and an older man who donated this land to the Appalachian Trail Conservancy. He was a very interesting individual and knew the entire history of this part of Maine.

## 2019 Boise-Cascade Logging Road Northbound to Moxie Pond
## Sunday, July 21st – One Day Hike
## Day Fourteen of Seventeen Days

After completing two hard days around Saddleback Mountain, near Rangeley Maine, we chose to hike these next two sections as day hikes. I left my Subaru at Moxie Pond the afternoon before as there is limited parking near the AT. (GPS 45.2497,-69.8310) The access road is off Maine Highway Sixteen (ME 17) and north of Bingham Maine. The latter part of the access road is very rough and at times the pond water level is almost at road level. We had lots of pot holes to navigate around. This access road would be an even more difficult drive after a rain. We got a shuttle drop from the Caratunk House to the Boise-Cascade Logging Road today as the price was right and there is limited parking on this road.

We started north around 9:53 A.M. on a cloudy and overcast day. We had a somewhat steep climb of eleven-hundred (1100) feet over the next one-point-eight (1.8) miles. Rain was in the forecast today and we barely had time to put on our pack covers before a very heavy rain soaked through our clothes. The trail quickly became a river and my Gore-Tex Asolo boots got wet. By the time we got to the top of Pleasant Pond Mountain the rain had stopped and my hiking pants started to dry off, but not my soaked boots. I should have stopped and changed socks at the time and I realized later that was a big mistake. We had a long fourteen-hundred-foot (1400) descent over the next nearly five (5) miles, and at times it was very steep. I had to sit and slide over some of the steep drops as I couldn't take the chance on slipping and falling. I ripped the seat of my old hiking pants, but didn't realize it until we finished around 3:43 P.M. We had covered the six-point-seven (6.7) miles in just over six (6) hours, a good pace for seniors. I didn't waterproof my boots prior to hiking in Maine this year. I won't make that mistake again.

After we got back to The Caratunk House, I asked Paul if he had a boot drier and he said it was broken. I tried drying my boots on the hood of my car and I was lucky that I had my older Asolo boots with me in my Subaru as a backup.

**2019 Sunday, July 21st, 8:05 A.M. – Moxie Pond young moose photo taken through Subaru window**

## 2020 Bald Mountain Road Southbound to Moxie Pond South End Road
## Monday, July 13th – One day hike
## Day Five of Sixteen Days

July 2020 would be my last section hike to complete Maine's two-hundred eighty-one-point-eight (281.8) AT miles. My first AT hike in Maine was in September 2009 with a failed attempt at Katahdin. I was sixty-eight (68) years young then, and I'm seventy-nine (79) years young now with lots of trail experience and also with lots of mistakes that I've made during these past eleven (11) years.

Poet, the co-owner at Shaw's in Monson, shuttled us to Bald Mountain Road at 8:05 A.M. He had arranged for us to eat breakfast at 6 A.M. today (normally Shaw's doesn't serve breakfast until 7 A.M.) and we left Shaw's around 6:50 A.M. There isn't any place to park near the AT as Bald Mountain Road is a gravel road and is barely one and a half cars wide and no shoulders. We started our ford of Bald Mountain stream at 8:05 A.M. The water was very cold and the rocky bottom was covered with very slick rocks. My ViaVia Barefoot water shoes worked well, but I did have a few slight slips as I slowly waded across the stream. I always unbuckle my hip belts and chest straps just in case I fall. That makes it easy to get your pack off and not be dragged downstream by the stream's current. The cold water felt great on my feet and I always carry a small compact towel to dry off my feet. We were ready to continue hiking south by 8:20 A.M.

The trail was pretty flat and the roots not too big for this part of Maine. We reached Moxie Bald Mountain Lean-to around 9:36 A.M. but chose not to stop. Over the next two hours and one-point-eight (1.8) miles we climbed fourteen-hundred (1400) feet up to Moxie Bald Mountain. The climb was pretty easy compared to the other mountains we had climbed in Maine.

This is also not a place I'd want to be if it rained, and it did look like it would rain later today.

**2020 Saturday, July 10, 2021, 2:40 P.M. Old Blue Mountain – minor injury – photo by Chill**

**2020 Monday, July 13th, 11:56 A.M. Moxie Bald Mountain GrandPa Walking – photo by Chill**

We hiked down thirteen-hundred (1300) feet over the next two miles and got to the turn off to Bald Mountain Brook Lean-to just as it started to rain. We walked as fast as we could and got to the Lean-to and arrived just before the downpour started. I didn't check my watch but it was at least forty-five (45) minutes before the rain stopped and we could continue our hike.

During the downpour, it was great to just sit in a dry Lean-to and snack. We just waited for the rain to stop. It felt good to have this break today. From Bald Mountain Brook Lean-to we had a fairly easy descent of three-hundred (300) feet to Baker Stream. I sent a text message from my Garmin inReach Explorer+ to Chill's wife and Madeleine that we still had two miles to hike today. The water level was very low and we were able to rock hop my last stream crossing in Maine. We got to my Subaru at 4:40 P.M. having hiked ten-point-eight (10.8) miles in just over ten (10) hours. This was a great pace, especially since we had to wait point-seven-five (.75) hours until the rain stopped. I drove us back to Shaw's and I ate my last AT dinner in Maine at Shaw's Hiker Hostel with Joker and Chill.

**2020 Monday, July 13th, 5:30 P.M. picked up rock on Moxie Pond Road near where my Subaru was parked – GrandPaWalking last Maine AT mile – Madeleine painted the rock for me in December 2020**

2020 Tuesday, July 14th, 8:25 A.M. Shaw's Hiker Hostel, Monson Maine
Poet, Chill, and Hippy Chick – Poet and Hippy Chick Co-owners

## 2016 Bald Mountain Road Northbound Shirley-Blanchard Road
### Tuesday, August 31st – One Day Hike
### Day Ten of Ten Days

Ed, now Joker, and I had been hiking the Hundred Mile Wilderness in Maine and I felt I needed a couple of easier day hikes. We were told there was no parking at Bald Mountain Road so we got a shuttle drop from Shaw's in Monson. We started north around 8:50 A.M. The trail was quite easy compared to the Hundred Mile Wilderness and we made great time. Our first ford was West Branch of Piscataquis River, at the two-mile mark, and I decided not to risk rock hopping and changed into my ViaVia Barefoot shoes. The water was cold but still felt great. Joker snacked while I changed back into my boots. We had a few ups and some were a bit steep but nothing was too hard today. The Horseshoe Canyon Lean-to was four-hundred (400) feet off the trail but we didn't stop. We both rock hopped the last stream and had our last climb after crossing a gravel road. We were back at my Subaru by 1:55 P.M. The MATC parking area is about two-hundred (200) feet from the AT.

We had hiked seven-point-seven (7.7) miles in just under four (4) hours. Our nearly two-mile-per-hour pace was great for us. We stayed at Shaw's in Monson again tonight.

### 2016 Shirley-Blanchard Road Northbound
### Maine Highway Fifteen (ME 15), Monson
### Monday, August 30th – One day hike
### Day Nine of Ten Days

We drove from the AT Lodge in Millinocket to Monson this morning. I found the AT parking area and with Joker's help I backed into a spot next to another car. We headed up the road to the AT and started hiking north at 11:05 A.M. We had a small climb initially and then a couple of other smaller climbs up to around thirteen-hundred-eighty-nine (1389) feet. The AT dropped a bit between the last gravel road and Maine Highway Fifteen (ME 15) where we finished at 2:57 P.M. We had hiked these six-point-three (6.3) miles in under three-point-five (3.5) hours. We stayed at Shaw's in Monson tonight.

### Summary

July 2019 two-days, one Lean-to night; two day hikes;
July 2020 one day hike;
August 2016 two day hikes;

Six hikes, Seven hiking days, Fifty-seven (57) miles, Average eight-point-one-four (8.14) miles per day.

# Chapter Seven
## Hundred Mile Wilderness Monson to Baxter State Park

The Hundred Mile Wilderness in Maine is the longest stretch of the AT without a major road crossing. The roads the AT crosses are logging roads and some are private roads that require an entrance fee in "**cash**". Most Maine State highways are at least ten or more miles from these access roads. Among the roads that access the AT near Monson, is Bodfish Farm/Long Pond Tote Road which isn't drivable for most vehicles. Otter Pond parking is about point-eight (.8) miles from the AT and is a narrow rutty but drivable road. The next access point is Katahdin Iron Works Road that connects to Maine Highway Eleven (ME 11) or Maine Highway Six (ME 6) north of Greenville.

    KI Road as it is known is private and a cash fee is required to enter. It's free if you are over seventy. The KI Road also gives you access to Johnson Pond Road (GPS 45.615697,-69.128794) and Jo-Mary Road (GPS 45.6506,-69.0307). There are two Appalachian Mountain Club (AMC) Lodges near KI Road. The AMC Gorman Chairback Lodge and Cabins is about a half-mile from the Third Mountain Trail. Little Lyford Lodge and Cabins is about a fifteen-minute drive from the

Gorman Chairback Lodge. There is also an access road to White House Landing off the Golden Road. AWOL's *AT Guide* also lists the Gravel Road near south end of Nahmakanta Lake (GPS 45.8824,-69.0317); Pollywog Stream (GPS 45.7796,-69.1720); and Abol Bridge on the Golden Road (GPS 45.8352,-68.9693) in his *2021 AT Guide*.

It is my recommendation that you consider purchasing a detailed road map of Maine. I recommend "The Maine Atlas and Gazetteer by DeLorme". GPS works well in Maine but can take you down logging roads that have been abandoned or seldom used. Sticking to the Maine highways to access the side and logging roads is your safest bet.

## 2013 Maine Highway Fifteen Northbound
## Bodfish Farm/Long Pond Tote Road
## Friday, July 19th – Saturday, July 20th –
## Two-day, one Lean-to night
## Days One and Two of Two Days

This was supposed to be a three- or four-day backpack to Katahdin Iron Works Road. This was the first time I realized my Garmin Nuvi 500 GPS would not be effective in this part of Maine as the GPS thinks all logging roads are drivable. The three (Harold, David and I) of us decided to arrange for a pick up at Katahdin Iron Works Road. Hiking to a shuttle pick up is a bad idea and I learned that in the future we would always hike to one of our cars at our end point. My Rule 22. Except for my failed attempt at Katahdin in September 2009 and my success in July 2011 in completing my missing miles to Baxter Peak on Katahdin, I had little experience with the difficult and rugged terrain in Maine. All I knew was that Maine is rugged and tough and there would be no easy hiking on Maine's AT.

We headed north from Maine Highway Fifteen (ME 15) on this hot and humid Friday in July. We started at 8:30 A.M. and although the terrain looked sort of level, we had a series of short ups and downs over the first three miles. We took a break at Leeman Brook Lean-to but David with his long legs decided to hike on ahead. This was another mistake I would avoid in the future. In Maine you and your hiking partners should always be in sight of one another or have an agreed upon time to stop for breaks. The heat and humidity were starting to affect me. The rain had left everything wet and with the high humidity today the slate rocks were like walking on ice. I didn't know how slippery slate rocks were at that time. As I hiked down to Little Wilson Stream I slipped on a large slab of slate rock and landed very hard on my back. My backpack broke my fall. At the time I felt okay. I took off my boots and socks and forded the stream. We stopped after we had forded Little Wilson Stream to refill and purify the water. I drank almost two liters of water and then refilled my Platypus with two liters. I also drank the entire twenty (20) ounces from my Gatorade bottle. I was tired and exhausted but we still had three-point-six (3.6) miles to hike to Wilson Valley Lean-to. As we climbed up the trail after crossing the stream I slipped again, hitting my shoulder on either a rock or tree stump and skinned my right knuckle. I slipped again on wet moss but landed on my knees. I was lucky this time.

By the time we had gotten to Big Wilson Stream, two-point-nine (2.9) miles later, I wasn't sure I could ford this stream. David was there and directed us to cross about fifty (50) yards upstream from where a rope had been strung across the stream. He was a big help and the water was very shallow in the place he directed us to cross. In spite of being tired, the cold water felt great, but I took my time crossing. I slipped several times and came close to falling twice.

After drying my feet and putting my boots back on, I used my SteriPen to purify another two liters of water, drank it all down and purified another two liters.

The AT was steep and muddy and David had found another trail parallel to the AT but it was several hundred feet down the railroad tracks. We followed the tracks and then climbed about a hundred (100) feet to where we were back on the AT. This part of the trail to Wilson Valley Lean-to wasn't as steep or muddy. It was nearly 7 P.M. when we got to Wilson Valley Lean-to. It had taken us eleven (11) hours to hike ten-point-four (10.4) miles. I was not only exhausted but chaffed too. I applied Body Glide and felt a lot better. After dinner I called Shaw's on my cell and they answered.

Cell service in most of Maine is not reliable and I got lucky today. I knew I would not be able to hike much tomorrow and after some discussion about where I could hike out, Shaw's suggested Bodfish Farm/Long Pond Tote Road. They told me the road from the AT came out to a gravel road and near a concrete bridge. I'd have to hike northbound about three-point-eight (3.8) miles to Bodfish Farm/Long Pond Tote Road and they said it would be about another mile or more out to the gravel road. We agreed on a 2 P.M. pick up as that would give us six (6) hours to get to the pickup point.

I tried to lay down but the pain in my lower back was sharp and severe. I could barely lay on my back and turning over was also very painful. I had passed a kidney stone earlier this year and still had the Percocet pills that I used when I passed the kidney stone. I took one Percocet and about thirty (30) minutes later I was out for most of the night. At least I got some sleep tonight.

## 2013 Wilson Valley Lean-to Northbound
## Bodfish Farm/Long Pond
## Tote Road to Gravel Road Pickup
## Saturday, July 20th – Day Two of Two

I was up by 5:30 A.M. and David was already up. I still felt exhausted and my back still hurt, and I wasn't sure if I could carry my full pack. Harold offered to carry most of my food and my sleeping bag as these were the items that weighed the most. We left the Lean-to just before 7 A.M. and although it was cooler today, the humidity was still quite high. We had seven hours to get to our pick-up point. We had several short but steep downs and I wasn't surprised I didn't fall. I did sit down and slide down some of these descents. Carrying a much lighter pack felt good, but my lower back still ached. We made good time and got to where the AT connected to Bodfish Farm/Long Pond Tote Road ahead of schedule.

We took off our packs, sat down, snacked, and discussed our options. I told David and Harold last night and again this morning that I was going to hike out the Tote Road. I said I would arrange to have them picked up at Katahdin Iron Works Road if they wanted to continue hiking north. Apparently Harold had some chaffing issues yesterday and today and he was ready to call it quits. I told David that if he wanted to hike onto KI Road, I'd pick him up. They both decided to hike out with me. I was told it was "about a mile" to the gravel road and I soon found out "about a mile" in Maine can actually be a lot more than a mile and more likely two miles.

We had a small shallow stream to cross and I decided not to take off my boots and I just waded through. David and Harold stopped to take off their trail shoes. As I hiked down the muddy and pot-holed water-filled road, I realized this road had not been maintained in years. I got to one water-filled pot hole that covered the entire width of the road. I started to wade through, and the water was now over my boots, then up to my knees. At this point I told myself that if the water goes over my knees I will turn around and bushwhack around this huge water-filled pot hole. The water dropped below my knees and I continued until I was back on the muddy road. Looking back I guessed I had walked over a hundred-fifty (150) feet through this muddy water. There were more water-filled pot holes, but none were very deep and some I could just walk around the edge. Just beyond the last water-filled pot hole I could see the gravel road. I realized this was the road my Garmin tried to take me down the day before.

 David and Harold were about ten-minutes behind me and by the time they arrived I had taken off my boots and put on clean and dry socks. Yes, my boots were soaked but my feet were a little drier. A lady came by and offered us a ride into Monson, but I said we were waiting for our shuttle from Shaw's. The shuttle arrived about forty-five (45) minutes later and it was a short ride back to Shaw's. I put my pack in the back of my Subaru and grabbed some clean clothes and headed to the showers on the second floor at Shaw's. After I showered I noticed the bruises on my shoulder and my ribs but couldn't see anything on my back. David had forgotten to lock his car on Friday when we left and most of his food was gone. He was upset and left for his Maine campsite. Harold and I spent the night in the large bunk room on the second floor and then we headed home on Sunday, July 21st. This was one of the only times I didn't take any photos on an AT section hike. I'm not sure if David or Harold did either.

## 2017 Otter Pond Parking to AT South to Bodfish Farm Long Pond Tote Road – Wednesday, August 30th, One day hike Day Twelve of Twelve Days

Ed (now Joker) and Jim (now Chill) had planned to backpack southbound Wednesday, August 30th and Thursday, August 31st from where Otter Pond Parking meets the AT southbound to Monson over two days. On Tuesday, August 29th, after our two-day, one Lean-to night we stopped for lunch on our way back to Shaw's. During lunch, Chill broke a tooth and after speaking with his dentist decided to head home the next day. I decide to day hike with Joker southbound to where Long Pond Tote Road crosses the AT.

We didn't start until 9:10 A.M. because Joker forgot to take my Pocket Rocket stove and canister and ATC terrain map and we had to hike back to my Subaru to get them. The AT terrain was pretty easy as we headed southbound but then the trail became very narrow and slanted down towards the stream below. It was 10:18 A.M. when Joker rock hopped across the stream and headed south. Poet, co-owner of Shaw's in Monson, told me about a shortcut back to the parking area marked by pink ribbons in the trees. I followed the ribbons and I was back at my Subaru by 10:30 A.M. I drove my Subaru back down the gravel road and across a concrete bridge and parked on the gravel road near Bodfish Farm/Long Pond Tote Road. I took my daypack along with a twenty-ounce Gatorade and my partially filled Platypus and started hiking to where the AT intersects this road. The road was somewhat in better shape, but there were pot holes and a couple of places where it looked like a large truck had slid off the road. The road split (this was a single road back in 2013) and it looked like the road on the right was the original road. I took it and followed it to the AT and then hiked the AT to the side of the stream Joker had rock hopped earlier. As I was about to turn around and head back, I noticed a middle aged guy coming across the stream Joker had rock hopped. He seemed to be struggling so I waited until he was on my side of the stream. I asked him if he was hiking south and he said he was hiking north. He said he didn't realize how difficult the AT was since he left Monson and was looking to bail. I told him that I had a car about one-point-five (1.5) miles away and I'd give him a ride to Shaw's in Monson. He asked what Shaw's was. He kept trying to get through on his cell but he couldn't connect. He followed me south on the AT to the second road and then back down the Tote Road to my Subaru.

The second or newer road connected to the Tote Road just past a small shallow stream. I drove him back to Shaw's and during our short drive he told me his truck was at Katahdin Iron Works Road. He wasn't familiar with AWOL's *AT Guide* and didn't have an emergency beacon on his very large pack. When we arrived at Shaw's I suggested he speak with Poet about getting a ride to his truck. It was apparent he was not prepared for this part of Maine and wasn't aware of any of the access trails. After I dropped him at Shaw's I spoke with Poet about his situation and then started my drive back to Annapolis.

Note: If I had to hike this again, I would have broken it up into two days. Day One, Maine Highway Fifteen (ME 15) to Wilson Valley Lean-to & Day Two Wilson Valley Lean-to to Otter Pond Parking.

### 2017 Otter Pond Park to AT – Northbound to Katahdin Iron Works Road
### Friday, August 25th – Tuesday, August 29th –
### Two, two day, one night backpacks and One Zero Day
### Days Seven and Eight – Zero Day Nine –
### Days Ten and Eleven of Twelve Days

I had studied these nearly fifteen AT miles and they not only looked rugged, but had a lot of steep and rugged terrain. I really didn't want to carry a full pack for three days and two nights. In August of 2016 while I was staying at Shaw's with Joker, I asked Poet if there was a way to break up these miles and he said "Use the Third Mountain Trail" and he showed it to me on his wall map of the AT. He also told me about an AMC Lodge that was about a half-mile from the base of the Third Mountain Trail. My dilemma for our 2017 hiking was nearly solved.

On Friday, August 25th, we started up the point-eight (.8) miles from Otter Pond parking at 8:08 A.M. to the AT. This trail was steep in part and I almost missed its intersection with the AT as another hiker was sitting right at the junction and I didn't see a sign nor a white blaze. Joker, Chill, and I had a tough and very steep climb of nine-hundred (900) feet over the next mile with the grade greater than twenty-five-percent (25%) at times. I lost count on the number of times I stopped to catch my breath. After passing Barren Ledges we had another seven-hundred-foot (700) climb over the next one-point-eight (1.8) miles to Barren Mountain. We rested at the sight of the old tower. The descent to the turn off to Cloud Pond Lean-to wasn't too hard, but the point-four-mile (.4) side trail to the Lean-to was filled with rocks and large roots. We'd covered the three-point-eight (3.8) AT miles and one-point-two (1.2) non-AT miles in just under five (5) hours. Cloud Pond Lean-to sat above the pond which was our water source and we'd have the place to ourselves tonight.

It was in the mid-forties when we woke up on Saturday, August 26th, and I had trouble getting warm. We left the Lean-to around 7:45 A.M. and got back to the AT around 8 A.M. The trail seemed easier this morning. The trail descended five-hundred (500) feet over the next one-point-five (1.5) miles, but the large roots and rocks made for slow progress. The Fourth Mountain Bog was muddy and we had to be careful on the bog boards, as many of them were in bad shape and the mud was deep in spots. At one point my left trekking pole was nearly a foot into the mud and it hadn't hit bottom. The point-six-mile (.6) climb up Fourth Mountain wasn't too steep but rocky. We stared down our soon-to-be descent of Fourth Mountain and all I thought was that I was looking down a Colorado or Utah double black diamond ski run without snow. It was very steep but the rocks were like blocks and we all just took our time climbing down. We had one shorter climb up Mount Three and a Half to the Third Mountain Trail.

It was about 12:30 P.M. when we started down the Third Mountain Trail, a groomed and sort of easy trail down to my Subaru at the base of this trail. We arrived at 1:35 P.M. having hiked the three-point-seven (3.7) AT miles and the additional three (3) non-AT miles over six-point-five (6.5) hours. We spend the night at Little Lyford AMC Lodge in the bunkhouse. Sunday, August 27th, was our Zero Day and except for another couple we had the entire Lodge to ourselves. We had planned to stay at the AMC Lodge which was closer to Third Mountain Trail on Saturday, the 26th, but the AMC crew took over the bunk room. There had been an incident in which one of the crew had died. We didn't ask about the details as it was none of our business.

**2017 Friday, August 25th, View from Barren Mountain –
photo by Joker**

On Monday, August 28th, we left the parking lot on KI Road at 8:41 A.M. and we were hiking south by 9:09 A.M. The first part of the trail was sort of easy but from the intersection of the AT and the trail to East Chairback Pond up Chairback Mountain was very steep and rugged. It was a very hard and tough climb of six-hundred (600) feet over the next two-point-one (2.1) miles. Chairback was sort of like Fourth Mountain but the stone blocks were larger and much harder to climb. I ended up zig zagging to find the easiest way up. Chairback Lean-to was about a half-mile from the top of Chairback Mountain and we arrived just after 1:10 P.M. We had hiked the three-point-eight (3.8) AT miles and the side trail miles into the Lean-to in just over five-point-seven-five (5.75) hours. Tonight, we would again have the Lean-to to ourselves.

**2017 Monday, August 28th, 1:19 P.M.
Joker climbing Chairback Mountain**

On Tuesday morning August 29th, we were up early and left Chairback Lean-to around 7:37 A.M. We had one short but steep climb of three-hundred-fifty (350) feet up to Columbus Mountain over the next point-three (.3) miles and then a long five-hundred-fifty-foot (550) descent to the turn off to West Chairback Pond over the next one-point-three (1.3) miles. The trail then climbed two-hundred (200) feet over the next point-six (.6) miles to Third Mountain and Monument Cliff. We had point-six (.6) miles further to hike before we were heading back down the Third Mountain Trail to Chill's rental. We arrived at 11:54 A.M. having hiked three-point-two (3.2) AT miles and then two (2) miles of the Third Mountain Trail in four-point-five (4.5) hours. We had a nice lunch on our way back to Shaw's in Monson. Chill broke a tooth at lunch and would head home on Wednesday, August 29th to see his dentist.

**2017 Tuesday, August 29th, 10:22 A.M. – GrandPa Walking Shadow on bog board**

## 2016 Katahdin Iron Works Road to Gravel Road near south end Nahmakanta
### Sunday, August 21st through Saturday, August 27th

Although 2013 was my first hike in the Hundred Mile Wilderness, by 2016 I had a lot more experience and had learned not to underestimate the difficulties of hiking in Maine. I had spent a considerable amount of time learning about the various logging roads and had obtained detailed maps of most of the logging roads between KI Road and Golden Road (near Millinocket). AWOL's *AT Guide* in 2016 had Johnson Pond Road mislabeled as Kokadjo B Pond Road. The mistakes I had made between 2009 and 2015 had been excellent teaching moments.

### Sunday, August 21st through Wednesday, August 24th 2016
### Days One through Four of Ten Days

On Sunday, August 21st, around 9:32 A.M. our shuttle driver, Duffy, dropped us on KI Road right on the AT and we started backpacking northbound for the next three days. The West Branch of Pleasant River was a half-mile from where we were dropped and it was over two-hundred (200) feet wide with no rocks to rock hop. I used my ViaVia Barefoot water shoes to cross the river. The water never got above my calves.

**2016 Sunday, August 21st, 10 A.M. – GrandPa Walking ford of the West Branch of Pleasant River – photo by Joker**

After drying off, we climbed four-hundred (400) feet over the next two (2) miles. This climb was easy compared to what we had hiked south of East Flagstaff Road southbound to the Maine New Hampshire Border, but hiking with a full pack (approximately twenty-four pounds) made the climb harder. We passed the Gulf Hagas cut-off trail and continued north and climbed nine-hundred (900) feet over the next three (3) miles. Joker and I arrived at Carl A Newhall Lean-to around 2:06 P.M. and Pokey arrived a few minutes later. We had hiked six-point-one (6.1) miles in three-point-five (3.5) hours. We were hiking to my Subaru at Johnson Pond Road where our shuttle driver had picked us up earlier this morning and then shuttled us back to KI Road. The cost was great, as we split the cost three ways and didn't have to drive back to get a second vehicle at KI Road.

On Monday, August 22nd, we left Carl A Newhall Lean-to around 8:32 A.M. Over the next two (2) miles we climbed nearly thirteen-hundred (1300) feet over rocky terrain with huge roots. We took a short break on West Peak. We had a series of climbs and descents but the AT was mostly up over the next one-point-six (1.6) miles. Just after the White Brook Trail we started our final seven-hundred-foot (700) climb up White Cap Mountain. It was very windy and reminded me of hiking southbound from Mount Washington to Madison Spring Hut in the White Mountains of New Hampshire. The trail was like the rocks during my last two (2) miles of climbing Katahdin. I took my time and stopped a few times between wind gusts just to make sure of my footing on this jumble of rocks.

2016 Monday, August 22nd, 2:50 A.M. –
Joker hiking down from White Cap Mountain

2016 August 22nd, 10 A.M. –
Dense Maine woods on either side of the AT

We hiked down thirteen-hundred (1300) feet over the next one-point-four (1.4) miles on rock steps that had been placed to cut down on erosion. Really wished we had these rock steps on the last climb up. We arrived at Logan Brook Lean-to around 3:45 P.M. having hiked seven-point-two (7.2) miles in four-point-five (4.5) hours. Looking back, the four large climbs today and the constant up and down had worn me out.

Tuesday, August 23rd was our third backpacking day and I was looking forward to a hot shower and real bed tonight. We left Logan Brook Lean-to around 7:01 A.M., and over the next three-point-six (3.6) miles the trail descended eleven-hundred-fifty (1150) feet. Just past East Branch Lean-to we forded the East Branch of the Pleasant River where a gust of wind took my favorite wide brim hiking hat. I saw it float downstream and out of sight. The trail was somewhat muddy but large roots were the main obstacle and I had to take my time.

We had a nice but short walk along the sandy beach of Mountain View Pond followed by a four-hundred-foot (400) climb over the next one-point-six (1.6) miles up Little Boardman Mountain. From Little Boardman Mountain we had a very easy descent of seven-hundred-fifty (750) feet over the next one-point-three (1.3) miles to Johnson Pond Road and my Subaru. It was 2:23 P.M. and we had hiked eight-point-four (8.4) miles in under five-point-five (5.5) hours. I drove us back to Millinocket and the Paloma Motor Lodge. It was great to take a long hot shower and put on clean clothes and eat real food.

Wednesday, August 24th was our fourth consecutive hiking day, but our first day hike. Joker, Pokey and I were joined by Emilio who had driven up from Washington, D.C. the night before. I drove my Subaru with Emilio and Pokey drove her vehicle with Joker from Millinocket south on Maine Highway Eleven (ME 11) to Jo-Mary Road (a private logging road). Being over seventy, Pokey and I didn't have to pay the

$10 cash fee but we still had to register our cars. Pokey followed me down Jo-Mary Road to the junction of Johnson Pond Road. We got in each other's cars, Emilio riding with me and Joker riding with Pokey and I drove Pokey's vehicle to where we had parked when we finished yesterday. She and Joker would be hiking southbound and Emilio and I would be hiking northbound.

**2016 August 24th, 8:15 A.M. Yup, this is the AT in Maine**

We started at 7:48 A.M. and had an easy hike except for crossing over a jumble of wood sticks and logs. Around 9:28 A.M. and just past Cooper Brook Falls Lean-to we came upon Phil Tymon, who was using a broom to support himself as he hobbled north. He told us that a couple of days ago he had slipped while getting water from the brook and injured his ankle. His friend, a Thru Hiker, had continued north and Phil had spoken with "Old Man" at the AT Lodge in Millinocket about being picked up today at Jo-Mary Road. I told Phil that once I got to Jo-Mary Road I would drive Emilio back to Millinocket and then come back and pick him up.

We met Pokey and Joker heading south just a few minutes later and I told them about Phil and my plans to come back and pick him up. I wasn't thinking and made a big mistake! What I should have done was to tell Pokey to wait for me at where Jo-Mary Road and Johnson Pond Road meet. They could have taken Emilio with them back to Millinocket and I could have just driven back to Jo-Mary Road and waited for Phil. Isn't hindsight great? We hiked the mostly easy seven (7) miles in just a bit over three (3) hours.

I drove back to Millinocket, dropped off Emilio and stopped at the AT Café to pick up sandwiches for Phil and me. He called me to say he was close to Jo-Mary Road and I told him I was picking up sandwiches. I asked if he wanted white or rye, he said "Rye". I raced back down Maine Highway Eleven and only slowed down at the Check In place. I had to slow my speed to under 50mph on the gravel road as my Subaru was sliding a bit on this great gravel road. Phil was waiting for me as I drove up. He asked me if I had some paper as he wanted to leave a note asking any SoBo hiker to return the broom to Cooper Brook Falls Lean-to. He ate his sandwich, "on Rye" while I drove him back to Millinocket and the Emergency Room. I told him to call me after he saw the Doctor and I would drive him to wherever he needed to go. His Thru Hiker friend was expected to arrive at the AT Lodge either later today or tomorrow. We did hear that the "broom" got back to the Lean-to a few days later.

I picked Phil up several hours later and he told me he had broken his ankle and he couldn't stay at the AT Lodge as climbing two sets of stairs would be difficult. I suggested he consider Pamola Motor Inn where Joker, Pokey and I had stayed earlier in the week. I drove him there and introduced him to the Manager who had taken care of Joker and me earlier. Phil and I have stayed in touch via email and are Facebook friends. He would hike with me in September 2021 and help me complete my last AT miles in Vermont and Pennsylvania.

Joker and I stayed in a semi-private room at the AT Lodge and tomorrow would be our first Zero Day after backpacking for three days and day hiking a fourth day. Pokey decided to continue her hiking tomorrow and we wouldn't see her again. She would hike her last AT miles over the next several days and her AT would be completed. Joker and I agreed we needed the Zero Day.

Thursday, August 25th was our Zero Day and we arranged to have our laundry done at the AT Lodge. Emilio woke us up before 6 A.M. and said he was going to hike Katahdin. I just went back to sleep. Joker and I had a great breakfast at the AT Café (also owned by "Old Man") and an easy day with an early dinner at Scootic Inn. There is a pizza place just down the street from the AT Café which is excellent. We were in bed and around 9:30 or 10 P.M. Emilio knocked on our door and said he wanted to hike with us tomorrow. I said nothing and went back to sleep.

## 2016 Friday, August 26th – Saturday, August 27th – Days Six and Seven of Ten Days

We had left Joker's truck at Jo-Mary Road on Thursday. On Friday morning August 26th I drove Jo-Mary Road and followed my Garmin Nuvi 500 to the GPS location at the South End of Nahmakanta Lake (GPS 45.8824,-69.0317). We parked and Joker, Emilio and I headed southbound towards White House Landing. It was 8:48 A.M. when we finally started hiking. The terrain was pretty easy and mostly flat except for a few short and easy climbs. Emilio led and we had to stop a lot as he was a lot slower than when we hiked with him a couple of days earlier. It seemed he couldn't catch his breath. I also noticed he was sweating more than I'd ever seen him sweat. His pace was so slow that I started to lead and asked Joker kept an eye on him to make sure he didn't get too far behind. We covered the four-point-six (4.6) easy for Maine miles in two-point-seven-five (2.75) hours.

**2016 Friday, August 26th, 2 P.M. White House Landing**

As we waited for the boat to pick us up and take us to White House Landing, I noticed Emilio has sweated through his shirt and pants. I had serious concerns that his Katahdin hike yesterday had exhausted him. After we got to White House Landing and we were assigned our cabin I pulled Joker aside and said that I was concerned that Emilio would have an issue hiking the nearly ten (10) miles tomorrow and the climb up Potaywadjo Ridge. He had sweated through his pants and underwear and the chair he was sitting on was wet with sweat. I asked Joker to try and convince Emilio to get a ride back to Millinocket tomorrow morning as I didn't want to be responsible for his safety. We had a good dinner of cheeseburgers and my shower felt great. White House Landing was a great choice and allowed us to day hike for two days. I enjoyed sleeping in a real bed tonight.

On Saturday, August 27th, we had an excellent and filling breakfast before catching an early boat ride back to Mahar Tote Road. Emilio stayed at White House Landing to wait for a ride back to Millinocket. Joker and I started hiking around 8:34 A.M. Although AWOL's *AT Guide* shows a mostly level terrain, the Maine AT Terrain Maps also shows the trail to be mostly flat except for Potaywadjo Ridge. We had lots of large roots to contend with. We didn't stop at Potaywadjo Spring Lean-to, which was my Thirteen-Hundredth-Mile, but we did take a break at Antlers Campsite. We got back to my Subaru at 2:47 P.M., having hiked ten-point-three (10.3) miles in just a bit over five (5) hours. That was an excellent time for us seniors.

Emilio was at the AT Lodge when we arrived. We all had dinner together at the Scootic Inn, and Joker and Emilio had ice cream from a stand near the AT Lodge. Tomorrow would be another Zero Day and Emilio announced he'd be heading home.

Sunday, August 28th was a wonderful day to sleep in and then we had a late breakfast and just hung around Millinocket. Joker and I considered backpacking from Abol Bridge south to Nahmakanta Lake but I was tired and didn't want to carry a backpack for four days. Joker agreed with me and we decided to head south to Monson and day hike something easier for two more days. It would be August 2017 before we'd return to continue this part of the Hundred Mile Wilderness in Maine.

### 2017 Pollywog Stream – Katahdin Stream Campground, Baxter State Park
### Saturday, August 19th – Wednesday, August 23rd
### Day One through Five of Twelve Days

On Saturday, August 19th, Joker and I started day hiking southbound from Pollywog Stream (GPS 45.7796,-69.1720) to the South End of Nahmakanta Lake around 9:35 A.M. We had an initial steep climb of three-hundred (300) feet over a mile to Pollywog Gorge. We decided not to take the side trail to the Gorge. Over the next three-point-seven (3.7) miles we easily climbed up six-hundred (600) feet to Nesuntabunt Mountain. It was cloudy and we didn't get a good view of Katahdin. We climbed down nearly seven-hundred (700) feet over the next point-nine (.9) miles, but it wasn't as steep as I expected. Again, rocks and large roots were the big issues. We stopped at Wadleigh Stream Lean-to for a short back off rest break. Between the Lean-to and Nahmakanta Lake and my Subaru we had another very muddy trail. We finished the eight-point-six (8.6) miles in just over five (5) hours. It was 4:10 P.M. We had left my Subaru at Pollywog Stream as that would be our end point in three days. Joker drove us back to the AT Lodge in his truck for our overnight in a real bed.

**2017 Saturday, August 19th, 3:50 P.M. – Overcast beach walk**

On Sunday, August 20th, we had a short three-point-five-mile (3.5) backpacking day from the Golden Road. Our other choice was to hike fourteen-point-seven (14.7) miles from the Golden Road, but we felt that even with easier terrain those miles were just too much for us. Since we had only a few miles today, we didn't start until after 10 A.M. Except for large roots and some rocky parts, the trail and terrain were pretty easy. We finished in one-point-seven-five (1.75) hours and we had the entire Lean-to to ourselves tonight.

Tuesday, August 21st would be a very long twelve-point-five-mile (12.5) day. We left Hurd Brook Lean-to around 7:17 A.M. Over the next two-point-five (2.5) miles we climbed seven-hundred (700) feet of muddy and rocky terrain and on Rainbow Ledges we had an excellent view of Katahdin. The trail dropped nearly five-hundred (500) feet over the next one-point-eight (1.8) miles and we had an almost constant muddy and rocky trail. We were very tired by the time we crossed a narrow log bridge over Rainbow Stream and sat down in Rainbow Stream Lean-to. It was 3:38 P.M. and we'd hiked twelve-point-five (12.5) miles in six-point-five (6.5) hours. This was an excellent pace for us older guys in spite of the mud and rocky terrain.

2017 Sunday, August 20th 3:19 P.M. –
Hundred Mile Wilderness easier terrain

Joker and I discussed whether we should hike the remaining two-point-nine (2.9) miles or just spend the night. We were both very tired and since we didn't know what the terrain would be like, we decided to play it safe and spend the night at Rainbow Stream Lean-to.

**2016 Monday, August 22nd, 8:30 A.M. – stone steps
north side of White Cap Mountain**

On Wednesday, August 22nd, we left Rainbow Stream Lean-to at 8:14 A.M. The trail was narrow, slanted to the left and very muddy. There were lots of large roots and rocks to get around or over. I was happy we chose not to hike these miles yesterday. We still made good time, covering the two-point-nine (2.9) miles in a bit over ninety (90) minutes.

Joker and I agreed that had we hiked this yesterday it would have taken us a lot longer. I drove us to the Golden Road and we decided to hike the half-mile from where the AT comes out of Baxter State Park to where it enters the woods just past Abol Bridge on the Golden Road. I'm glad we did this today as it was hot and very humid, and the logging trucks that passed us threw up a lot of dust. We left my Subaru just off Golden Road when the AT enters Baxter State Park and Joker drove us back to the AT Lodge in his truck for our last night. Yup, we ate at Scootic Inn again tonight.

### Hundred Mile Wilderness Summary

2013 two-days, one Lean-to nights;
2017 one day hike; two two-day, two Lean-to nights;
2016 three-days, two Lean-to nights; one day hike; two-day, one Light House Landing night;
2017 one day hike; three-days, two Lean-to nights
Nine hikes, Seventeen hiking days, One hundred (100) miles, Average five-point-nine (5.9) miles per day

On Thursday, August 23rd, we decided to take the Old Man's 6:30 A.M. shuttle to Baxter State Park. He runs this shuttle most mornings and the cost is split among the number of riders. I think we paid ten dollars each today. We got to Baxter State Park just before 7 A.M. and checked in at the Ranger Station at Katahdin Stream Campground where we got our numbered check-in passes (#01691).

## 2017 Wednesday, August 23rd, 9 A.M. – Daicey Pond Baxter State Park

The AT from Katahdin Stream Campground to the Golden Road is in Baxter State Park and not the Hundred Mile Wilderness. The AT out of Baxter State Park is quite easy and mostly flat. We decided to take the blue blaze by-pass trail to avoid the rock hop across Nesowadnehunk Stream. Looking at the AT terrain map we saw we'd have to rock hop again back across Nesowadnehunk Stream again. The last part of the by-pass trail was steep but not muddy today. About a half-mile from the Golden Road we encountered swarms of gnats and I was glad I had applied my White Mountain Insect Repellant earlier. Joker had to put on his bug net as gnats love to fly into your eyes. I wore a pair of clear glasses like many dentists wear so my eyes were protected. Once we crossed the wooden footbridge and Katahdin Stream the gnats were gone. We hiked the nine-point-five (9.5) miles in four-point-five (4.5) hours and I was glad we had hiked that half-mile on the dusty Golden Road yesterday.

**2017 August 23rd, 1 p.m. – Golden Road Bridge over West Branch Penobscot River**

As I described in the beginning of Chapter One (pages 1-5), I had failed to complete Katahdin in September 2009 but completed my missing part in July 2011 with Ron Filbert my first hiking partner.

### 2011 Sunday, July 10th through Tuesday, July 12th
### Baxter Peak on Katahdin via Chimney Pond Campsite
### Day One through Three of Three Days

On Sunday, July 10th, 2011 Ron Filbert and I decided to take the non-AT trail from Roaring Brook Campground to Chimney Pond Campsite where we had reserved the Bunk House for two nights. The Bunk

House has two bunk rooms that sleep six each on bare wood platforms. We took the bunk room on the right. We got up early on Monday, July 11th, made breakfast, and began our climb up the Saddle Trail out of Chimney Pond to the Baxter Cutoff Trail. Around 8:36 A.M. just below our last climb onto the Baxter Cutoff Trail we put on warmer clothes and climbed up and onto the Baxter Cutoff Trail. There was a heavy fog and we carefully followed the Baxter Cutoff Trail towards Baxter Peak and the Katahdin sign. Ron almost took a wrong turn to our left that would have put him on the Abol Trail heading down. We arrived at Baxter Peak and then the Katahdin sign around 9:42 A.M. The top of Katahdin was still fogged in at 9:44 A.M. when we had another hiker take several photos of us.

**2011 Monday, July 11th, 9:44 A.M. – Ron Filbert and GrandPa Walking Katahdin near Baxter Peak – Baxter State Park, Maine**

By 10 A.M. the fog had cleared and I took a brief video of a clear three-hundred-and-sixty-degree view. Ron and I headed south down the AT to the Baxter Cutoff trail, past Thoreau Spring, to the "2M" mark on the rock. We then turned around and hiked back north to the Baxter Cutoff trail, turned left and took it towards the Saddle Trail. We got back to the Bunk House around 3 P.M. I was totally exhausted and was almost too tired to eat dinner. I also slept badly that night.

**2011 Monday, July 11th, 11:24 A.M. – Thoreau Spring junction of Hunt Trail and Baxter Cut-off Trail**

On Tuesday, July 12th, Ron and I headed back down the trail to Roaring Brook Campground and I noticed he was wearing his bug mask. He removed his bug mask once we got near Roaring Brook Campground and I noticed his face was swollen and one eye was almost swollen shut. We got some Benadryl from another hiker and I drove Ron to the Emergency Room. They treated Ron and the doctor told us some people have an allergic reaction to gnat bites in Maine. We spent the night in Millinocket as Ron could not drive and I didn't want to risk the long drive on my own this late in the day. The next day the swelling had gone down and both eyes were sort of normal but his face was still swollen. I drove us back to his home near Ocean City, Maryland and his wife was shocked at his appearance. I spent a few hours sleeping on his couch and then drove home to Crofton.

Ron and I had plans to hike again in 2012, but his skin cancer came back and he died in 2013. He was my first hiking partner and a great friend. He inspired me to find other hiking partners so I could continue my AT journey.

# Chapter Eight
## Conclusion and Statistics

For some Northbound or Southbound purists, you might find my descriptions confusing as we sometimes hiked Northbound and at other times Southbound depending on the terrain. Looking back, if I had to hike Maine again, I probably would not at my age. If I had started when I was five or ten years younger, I would definitely hike the southern part of Maine south of Flagstaff Road a lot sooner. I'd climb Katahdin next and arrange for a pick up at Roaring Brook Campground. I'd hike the hardest part of the Hundred Mile Wilderness between Monson and KI Road earlier along with the Hundred Mile Wilderness between KI Road to Johnson Pond Road. The rest of the Hundred Mile Wilderness from Baxter State Park south to Johnson Pond Road would be my next section to last section. My last section in Maine would be from East Flagstaff Road north to Monson.

| Year | Hikes | Days | Consecutive Days | Lean-to, Shelter, Tent Nights |
|---|---|---|---|---|
| 2009 | One | One | One | Two Lean-to |
| 2011 | One | Three | Three | Two Baxter State Park Bunk House |
| 2013 | One | Two | Two | One Lean-to |
| 2016 | Five | Eight | One, One, Three, One, Two | Two Lean-to, One White House Landing |
| 2017 | Four | Eleven | Two, One, Three, One, Two, Two | One Shelter, Four Lean-to |
| 2018 | Seven | Thirteen | Two, Three, Two, Two, One, Two, One | One Shelter, Five Lean-to |
| 2019 | Seven | Fourteen | One, Three, One, One, Two, Three, Two, One | One Tent, Three Lean-to, Two Shelter |
| 2020 | Three | Four | Two, Two, One | One Lean-to, One Tent |

**Totals**

Eight Seasons, 29 Hikes, 56 Days, 18 Lean-to, Two Baxter State Park Bunk House, One White House Landing, Four Shelter and Two Tent Nights.

Two-Hundred-Eighty-One-point-Eight (281.8) Miles – Average Five-point-Zero-Three (5.03) Miles per day. Including the Forty-Two-point-Seven-Five (42.75) Non-AT Miles, our average was Five-point-Eight (5.8) Miles per day.

I've hiked Maine with six seniors once each, one senior, Joker 2016 through 2020, and one senior, Chill 2017 through 2020.